D0175962

THE WORLD WAS HER CLASSROOM

by Roma Dehr

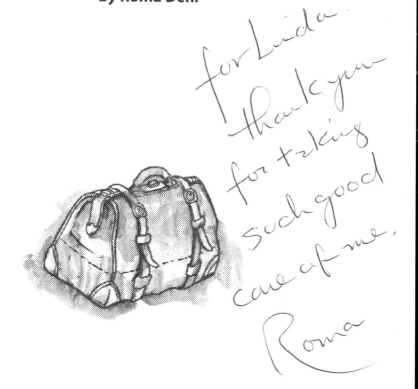

for Luda.
thank you
for taking
such good
care of me,

Roma

Published by AMC Media

For information or to order copies, contact:

USA
PMB 729
250 "H" Street
Blaine, WA
98230
800 667-6119

CANADA
1626 Trafalgar Street
Vancouver, BC
V6K 3R7

604 739-9345

Email: phonehome@shaw.ca

ISBN 0-919 597-21-1

Printed in Canada

Copyright 2004 by Roma Dehr
Cover art by Nola Johnston

All rights reserved. No part of this publication
may be used or reproduced in any manner
whatsoever without prior written permission
from the publisher.

Another Thor book

CONTENTS

INTRODUCTION

Our mother was propelled by three forces—knowledge, politics and adventure. From September to June, we attended public schools in Vancouver, British Columbia. After each school day, my sister and I came home to "school-after-school" where we learned to hold a pencil correctly, to read, and to memorize the times-tables months before our peers. Our mother made sure we attended marches for peace and the environment, gave to the poor and supported children in third world countries.

The day our summer vacations began our education was entirely in our mother's hands. She took us around the world to learn about and appreciate people in other cultures. During our travels my sister practiced reading and math, and I kept a journal of our adventures. As well, the three of us took hundreds of pictures in an effort to capture our adventures on film.

In preparation to write this book, my mother poured through my journals and sifted through tons of photographs. Then Zoe, mom and I spent time together rekindling our memories of those summers until my mother felt she had enough information to write this book. It was at that point she decided to use me as the storyteller. Her decision to use my voice was due in part to the fact that I had kept the journals and that our writing styles were so similar, and in part because our bold and adventurous mother is at heart a very shy person.

The pages that follow are a chronicle of these sometimes dangerous, always interesting adventures.

MY BIRTH

Our hearts stopped beating within seconds of each other. The same skilled hands that pulled me from my mother's womb and deftly removed the cord from around my neck moments later resuscitated my mother.

The crisis over, the nurses began to roll me out of the operating room in an incubator cart. "Macbeth," my mother called after me, "MacDuff was from his mother's womb untimely ripped."

"She named him Macbeth?" queried a nurse.
"Nope, Shakespeare I think," replied another.
"She named him Shakespeare?" asked the third.

She named me Thor. Thor Ché Dehr. Thor was a pretty big name for a full-term three-pound infant, but my mother emphatically assured everyone that I would grow into it. Che was of course after Ché Guevara, one of my mother's heroes. Many men had inspired her enough for me to bear their names—Thor Gandhi Dehr, Thor Galileo Dehr, Thor Da Vinci Dehr—but it was Ché whose name I would carry.

And what of my father? He left my mother on the day of my birth, and on that day her life changed radically as she ended the chapter on marriage, and began the next—life as a single parent.

THE SCHOOL BUS

I was three.

The happiest I have ever seen my mother was during the year and a half we spent living on a school bus. My mother's two great passions were her home and traveling, and the bus encompassed both. Its drab green exterior gave no hint of its exotic interior. The sounding board from a grand piano had been mounted just behind the driver's seat, perpendicular to the wall of the bus. Six short nails protruded from the top of the board near the ceiling. Attached to these nails hung strings of various lengths with horse chestnuts attached to them. As the bus rolled and pitched down the thousands of miles we covered, the horse chestnuts swung back and forth bouncing off the strings of the sounding board creating unique music in tune with the movement of the bus.

Our bus was 38 feet long. The back quarter was divided from the living space by a shingle-covered plywood wall. In the middle of the wall a cast iron door, that in a previous incarnation had served as the door of a very large wood-burning furnace, gave us just enough room to squeeze into the back storeroom. It was there that Michael slept, the tools were kept and the violins were stored.

Halfway up the plywood wall that separated the front part of the bus from the storage room, Peter, my mother's lover, had constructed a comfortable loft where he and my mother slept. He had cut a three-foot-diameter hole above their heads and installed a bullet- proof dome scavenged from a World War II fighter plane. A half-inch-diameter hole had been drilled into the apex of the dome.

My mother carefully crafted a cork to fit into that hole and hung a large multi-faceted crystal from it. Now, as the bus bolted and staggered down the road, the melody of the horse chestnuts was augmented by swirling rainbows that played on the walls, floor and ceiling. One would think that would be enough of a psychedelic experience for anyone, but my undauntable mother painted the inside of the bus chocolate brown which made the crystal rainbows even more pronounced.

On the left side of the bus, behind the driver's seat and between the sounding board and the sleeping loft, Peter installed a very small pot-belly stove. Opposite was a storage box three feet tall, two feet wide and four feet long. Its top was carefully padded and served as a seat by day and my bed by night. It was there, strapped in by a colorful Bolivian sash so I wouldn't roll off when the bus turned a corner, that I took my daily nap.

Since weight was no object when outfitting the bus, Peter chose a section of flooring from a bowling alley to fashion a countertop that ran from the storage box/bed to the loft. Jars of food, water buckets and bins containing our clothes were carefully strapped to shelves beneath the counter. Ancient Navajo rugs, instead of doors, protected them from sight. In an old junk store in Sedona, Arizona my mother found a row of six arched stained glass windows mounted on a board that was one foot tall and six feet long. Peter and Michael cut a hole in the side of the bus and installed them above the bowling alley countertop. I remember being mesmerized by the amber, green, blue, violet, crimson and indigo glass that cast their reflections on the velvet-smooth countertop.

One day something that had been carelessly left on the counter hit me on the head during my nap while we were traveling. My mother began an exhaustive search for something that could be mounted at the end of the counter as a small barrier to protect me from things that might roll off. I remember the day when Peter brought in a piece of iron sculpture featuring three crosses, a large one flanked by two smaller ones. "Just the thing," my mother cooed as she crossed herself and refrained from asking him where he had found it. I think we were in Colorado.

It took her a month to find just the right 6'x10' Persian carpet for the floor. The very next day, in a war veteran's thrift store in Albuquerque, New Mexico, she found yards of deep brown velvet to make window drapes. It was done. It was perfect. It was our home.

Peter

Peter, who would someday be the second man my mother would marry, did most of the driving. My mother sat by his side on a stool fashioned from the bottom of an old wooden swivel chair and a rusty tractor seat. I sat on her lap or played with Michael, the tools and the violins in the back room.

Peter fell in love with my mother the first day he saw her, eight years before I was born. At that time my mom was married to Richard Dehr, my father. Peter was seven years my mother's junior, and a good friend of my dad's younger brother. My mom paid little attention to the love-struck puppy who stared at her as inconspicuously as he could while at the same time dropping whatever was in his hands. My dad called her the Princess of Topanga, and was flattered by the attention she received from the young men. My mother hardly noticed Peter as my father was the center of her universe. Little did she know that eight years later she would be sitting at Peter's side on an 18-month road trip that would change her life forever.

Michael

Michael was 16 years old when he joined Peter on the school bus. Peter had met him the year before when Michael was living in Topanga Canyon with his parents and several foster children.

When Michael's family relocated to Marysville he did not do well. Michael was homesick for the friends and community he had learned to love. In Marysville his life took a turn for the worse. He began to make poor choices for himself and run with the wrong kids.

In what turned out to be a defining moment in Michael's life, Peter drove into town. He immediately saw that Michael needed some dramatic changes in his life including separating himself from his new friends. With Peter's uncanny ability for inserting himself into almost any situation with apparent ease, he convinced Michael's mother that Michael should leave Marysville and join him on the bus.

Michael traveled on the bus for over a year. It was a year that, in his own words, would reshape his life.

The Violins

A few days before we began our road trip, Peter and my mother put Peter's chainsaw in the trunk of his car and took it to a shop to have it sharpened. While waiting, Peter spied a child-sized violin behind the counter. The proprietor offered to sell it to him for $10. "Got any more?" asked Peter. The man was quick to say that he had ten more, and if we bought all ten he would lower the price to $8 each. "How many you got?" asked Peter. The man said that he had bought the defunct violin school next door so that he could expand his business and now was stuck with 200 violins that he was about to chop up for firewood. Peter offered him $500 for all of them. The man countered that he would sell them for no less than a thousand dollars. Peter pointed to the car we had driven up in, and they made a deal on the spot. Within minutes we had 200 violins and no car to take them home. My mother's frustration was soothed when Peter told her that he had traded a $300 guitar for the car a couple of weeks before.

A call to Michael, and within the hour our school bus pulled up and the violins were loaded in it. Peter and Michael spent the rest of that day making bins for the instruments with a sleeping pad on top of them that Michael shared with the toolbox. While they worked, my mother and I serenaded them with the horrific screeches that only absolute beginners can call forth from such a delicate instrument.

We headed north. Our first stop was a pawnshop in the city of Santa Barbara. Peter told my mother to go into the shop and pawn one of the violins. "What?" she stammered, "I don't know how to pawn anything. I don't even know how much money I should ask for." Peter told her that since we had purchased the violins for approximately $1.20 each, $10 would be a good price. My quivering mother, a violin clutched to her breast, entered the pawn shop. She told the man at the counter that the small violin was quite unique and had been hers as a child, but now that she had fallen on hard times she was ready to part with the little treasure. "How much?" responded the counter guy, who had heard it all, but who may have mistaken my mother's nervousness for quivers of grief.

My mother's mind went blank for a moment, and then she heard herself say, "fifty dollars."

"Forty-five," countered the man, who was puzzled when my mother abandoned the rare instrument on the counter and ran out the door. Moments later, she re-entered the store with a second violin.

"My brother's," she smiled.

"These damn things are getting a hell of a lot less rare," grunted the counter guy. "Eighty bucks for the pair of 'um." My mother hung her head, lovingly patted the violins, picked up the money and slowly walked out of the door. She broke into a run the second she hit the sidewalk, jumped into the bus and threw the money into the air. "We're rich," she yelled, " and we have 198 more violins back there!"

My mother, a high school teacher by profession and a socialist by persuasion, had never tasted true capitalism. Her first transaction in the marketplace made her heady with power, and with each sale her spirits rose, as did her ingenious ways of selling the violins. My socialist mother was on a roll. In Wyoming, after filling the 80-gallon gas tank Peter and Michael had installed under the bus, she approached the attendant and asked him if he had any small children at home. When the man said that he had two little girls, we all knew that he would soon be buying a violin. "Just look at this very precious little violin," she cooed, "can't you just see your darling little daughters playing it? Why I'll bet one of them is having a birthday sometime soon." He took the violin and we drove away with a full tank. My mother, however, giving in to proletarian guilt, returned an hour later and gave him a second one for his other daughter.

We sold, traded and gave away those violins for the next 18 months. Each transaction was filled with hippy imagination and the magic of our time together. My mother's last and most memorable sale occurred in a British Columbia antique shop where she sold what she called her "violin creation" for $250. She had bought an ornate old frame and a torn velvet skirt in a thrift shop in Oregon. In a drug store in Washington, she bought some shoe polish and a can of gold spray paint. She sprayed the frame gold, and covered the backing with a piece of the deep maroon velvet skirt. Then she buffed the violin with shoe polish and had Peter screw it onto the velvet backing. The knowledge that the dealer would double that price when he sold it delighted her, as did the image of the trail of violin-playing children that stretched across the continent behind our bus.

Learning to Read

Anyone who has had a teacher as a mother realizes they never stop teaching. My mother had been, and would always be, an ardent instructor. Just after my third birthday, she read the book *Teacher* by Sylvia Ashton Warner. It told of a woman who had taught Maori children to read by asking them what words they wanted to learn, and then using those same words to write books for them. The next morning my mother announced that it was time for me to learn to read.

"What word do you want to learn today?" she asked.

"Alligator," I answered. She wrote the word "alligator" on a 5x7 card and gave it to me.

"This is your word," she said. "Now go teach it to Peter and Michael." I did.

The words I chose on the following days were "giraffe," "Thor," "airplane," "OK," "glob," "bad," "peanut butter," "cried," "stop" and "good." As I had been instructed, I taught each word to Peter and

Michael and laughed when they mixed up "alligator" and "airplane." I could easily tell the difference between the two words because they looked different. In eleven days I had eleven words and my mother wrote and illustrated the following book for me to read:

"Once upon a time there was a Monster named Glob. Glob was a bad monster. Glob put peanut butter on an alligator. The alligator cried. Glob put peanut butter on a giraffe. The giraffe cried. The alligator and the giraffe cried and cried and cried. Then Thor came. Thor came in an airplane. Thor said "Stop Glob!" Glob did not stop. Thor put peanut butter on Glob, and Glob cried and cried and cried. "Will you stop?" Thor asked Glob. Glob said "yes." "Will you be good?" Thor asked Glob. Glob said "yes." "Good" said Thor. The alligator was good. The giraffe was good. Thor was good. Glob was good too. The End."

It was easy. I knew eleven of the words, and the rest I absorbed after my mother and I read the book together a few times. Peter and Michael seemed to take great delight in the story, and so I read it to them over and over and over again. A few days later the process began again, and soon I had many words and a series of books called *The Glob Stories*.

By the time I was ready to enter kindergarten I was reading on the third grade level. The glitch in Ms. Warner's system was that it produced wonderful readers and terrible spellers, as it did not teach how to break words down into their component syllables. My mother told me not to worry about spelling because someday someone would invent a machine that would check and correct my spelling for me. I believed my mother because she was my mother, because she was so passionate about things and because she was right most of the time.

Christmas

Christmas was coming, and my mother set herself the task of decorating the bus. We strung ropes of cranberries and strings of popcorn, and festooned them over the brown velvet drapes and the multicolored stained glass windows. My mother had perfected the art of making cookies by frying them in a skillet on our potbelly stove, and the cookie jar was full. With mounting anticipation, I looked at the stocking that hung on the stove's damper knob. My mother assured me that Santa would fill it on Christmas Eve. In preparation, she had read *The Night Before Christmas* every time I asked, and I asked a lot. I tried to imagine how Santa and his sled would come to the snowless desert outside of Flagstaff, Arizona, but my mother was so certain he would come that I stopped worrying about it.

My mother, however, began to worry. "It's the 24th, and I want to spend Christmas with my parents in California," she told Peter as she cut up vegetables for the stew she was making. "And so does Thor," she added as she chopped the potatoes with growing agitation. "We want a real Christmas, with a real fireplace and real presents." Peter's hesitation to make the 380-mile trip was due to a grinding sound that seemed to be coming from the transmission. It would be prudent to have the transmission checked by a mechanic before taking such a long trip, for losing a transmission in the middle of the desert could be both expensive and dangerous. But, one look at my mother's determined face convinced him to take the chance. We left that afternoon.

The stew was almost ready. Because it was too hot to have a fire in the potbelly stove, and because it was impossible to keep a pot on the stove while the bus was moving, my mother had made a cook box. She had learned about cooking in a box from an old English woman in Nevada. This type of cooking was not uncommon a hundred years ago in the English countryside. My mother's cook box deviated slightly from the old cook boxes as she used aluminum foil. First, she lined a large wooden box with foil, then she put a layer of fresh straw on the bottom. Next, she put in a covered pot that contained all the ingredients for the stew. She then packed more straw around and on top of the pot, lightly sprayed the straw with water and closed the box. The fermenting wet straw would emit enough heat to cook the stew within a day or two. Spontaneous combustion was definitely a problem, so every once in a while my mother would carefully lift the lid and let out some of the steam. It was tricky, but it worked.

15

The bus was decorated, my empty stocking was up, the stew was ready, and the cookie jar was full when we set out for my Grandma's house in California — the transmission making even more ominous sounds. True to form, Peter stopped for every hitchhiker he saw, and there were a lot of them. My mom said that Christmas was a hard time for many people and sometimes it made them restless. Soon, hitchhikers filled all the seats and were sitting on their packs on the floor. My mother passed out bowls of stew, and I gave them the Christmas cookies we had fried on the pot belly stove. Michael emerged from the back room with a cask of mulled wine that Peter had acquired by trading a violin, and everyone ate and drank and was happy. I told the hitchhikers that Santa was going to come that night and fill my stocking, and that I had to go to sleep in Michael's bed in the back room because they were sitting on mine. Everyone wished me a good night, and as I left they all began singing "Silent Night." I fell asleep almost immediately. Years later my mother told me what happened next.

When Peter tried to slow down to let a hitchhiker out, there was a great grinding sound. One of the hitchhikers, who had been a mechanic, told him that he had lost his first two gears. That meant that if Peter stopped the bus he would not be able to start it again. This presented a bit of a quandary, as we had nine hitchhikers who needed to leave before we reached Los Angeles. The best Peter could do was to slow down as much as he dared and let the hitchhikers throw their packs out the door and jump out after them. "Goodbyeeee," they called as they disappeared in the dark desert night. But before each of them left our bus they sifted through their packs and deposited a present in my stocking. Because people who hitchhike carry so little with them, each present bore a very special significance to its owner.

Peter, Michael, my mom and my sleeping self arrived in Los Angeles at five o'clock on Christmas morning. By some sort of miracle there were few cars and fewer policemen around, and Peter was able to drive through the red lights that stood between us and my grandparent's house. We pulled up to the house, stopped the bus and there it remained for three weeks until the transmission could be completely repaired.

The best part of my third Christmas was my stocking. It held wonderful surprises: a silver whistle, an ornate cross, a beautiful blue stone, a silver dollar, a small Bible, a photograph of a black and white dog, a yo-yo, a pocket knife with six blades, five pieces of candy and a pack of gum!

The Seventh Dayers

School buses are used for short runs. They pick up children and deliver them to the nearest school. Then they pick them up from school and return them to their homes. Peter and Michael drove our bus for hundreds of miles through the sweltering deserts of the Southwest, and over the mountainous continental divide and back again. The bus took a lot of punishment, and consequently it broke down all the time.

The routine seldom varied. When the bus broke down, Peter and Michael looked for a mechanic, preferably one who might be interested in child-sized violins, and my mother looked for work. It was the 70s and jobs were easy to find. In Sedona, Arizona she worked as a baker in a health food restaurant, in Albuquerque, New Mexico she worked as a sandal maker in a leather shop and in Dillon, Colorado she helped decorate a small ski chalet.

On the outskirts of Loveland, Colorado our bus began to make a hissing sound, and by the time we were able to pull over to the side of the road massive amounts of steam poured out from under the hood. My mother grabbed me and we rushed down the road to a large rock upon which we sat, fully expecting the bus to explode at any second. Eventually, the hood cooled down enough for Peter and Michael to open it. The news was not good. Michael suggested we had somehow overtaxed and ruined the radiator, and perhaps the "weight is no object" concept was flawed. Peter suggested that we shoot the bus in the headlight and leave it as a roadside monument. They returned to the steaming bus, and my mother and I sat on our rock and read my alphabet book.

While we were reading the alphabet the first time, we noticed a woman in a red truck drive by very slowly. She drove by again while we were reading the alphabet the second time. Just as we were beginning the alphabet for the third time, she drove up and stopped.

"How can I help you?" she called to my mother.

"My son and I would love a bath," my mother responded.

The woman looked at Peter and Michael and hesitantly asked, "Would just the two of you like to come to my house for a bath?"

"Oh yes, please," mom replied.

My mother ran back to the bus and gathered the garland of red chili peppers she and I had strung the previous day when the bus had broken down near a field of chilies. She told Peter and Michael that we were leaving with a nice lady in a red truck and we would be back in a little while. Peter told her there was no chance in hell they would be anywhere but there when she returned. With me in her arms and the garland of chilies, a gift for the woman, around her neck, my mother jumped into the Ford pickup and we drove away.

The woman introduced herself as a Seventh Day Adventist and told us her name was Lila. She said her husband's name was Lyle and they had six children whose names all began with the letter "L." Lila was a God-fearing woman who was a vegetarian, loved children and had married her high school boyfriend. My mother was a God-loving hippy who was a vegetarian, loved children and was traveling with a man to whom she was not married. The vegetables and the children won out over religious persuasion and marital status, and Lila and my mom became instant friends.

After we met the six "L" children, Lila led my mother and me into an immaculate bathroom that held a large, claw-footed tub, bottles of bath oil and bars of scented soap. While my mom and I were taking the best bubble bath in the world, Lila's husband Lyle came home.

Lila told him they had company, and that two of their guests were bathing and the other two were stranded on the highway. She politely asked Lyle to take his large John Deere tractor and gather the stranded guests.

I joined Lila's children and we all ran outside to see Lyle, Peter and Michael in the John Deere tractor pulling the green bus into the backyard. Lyle examined the radiator and confirmed that while Michael was correct, the radiator was indeed ruined, he quickly added that the engine was ruined as well. He said that Peter was correct as well, for without a knowledgeable mechanic and lots of money, the bus had no hope of being anything but a roadside monument. We had no mechanic and little money. It looked as if our travels had come to an abrupt end in Loveland, Colorado.

While Peter and Michael were showing my mother what had happened to our home on wheels, I opened the door of the bus and let the "L" children swarm through it. After a while, Lila and Lyle, who had been whispering to each other, approached Peter. Lyle told Peter he was a competent mechanic who preferred to work on motors than in his summer fruit stand. He said that he would be willing to work on the bus if Peter and Michael would work in his fruit stand. My mom sweetened the deal by offering to tutor the children who were having trouble with reading and math and by giving each of them a violin. A handshake later we began our lengthy stay with Lila and Lyle.

Sunday through Friday the routine was the same. We ate an early breakfast, then Peter and Michael drove Lyle's produce to his roadside stand and sold fruits and vegetables until dinnertime. Lyle busied himself fixing the bus, giving it an entire tune-up and waiting for spare parts to arrive by mail. Lila and my mother tended the children and, as Lila canned fruits and vegetables, mom taught Lucy and Linda to read and Lester his multiplication tables.

On Saturday, which is the seventh day for Seventh Day Adventists, we all went to church. Even though we must have seemed like heathens to the people in this small, religious community, they gave no indication that they feared us or felt any ill will toward us.

We were cordially invited to potlucks, summer strawberry parties and church picnics. The young girls wore their hair and their skirts long, and the entire community shunned dancing, soft drinks and coffee. They were all vegetarians. For some reason, our hippy band seemed to fit right in.

One morning, I awoke with a severe stomach ache and, after a series of home remedies that didn't work, Lila suggested that my mom take me to a doctor. We went to the Seventh Day Adventist hospital and were told that Lila's doctor was in a private hospital room. Before we entered, the nurse whispered to my mother that the doctor was dying. She said that even though he was quite ill he was still seeing patients. We entered the room with hesitation, and to our surprise found a most cordial healer in a hospital bed, surrounded by his wife and young daughters. He asked me to sit on the edge of his bed and gently examined me. When he was finished, he spoke at length with my mother about how to combine food so that a child who didn't eat meat would get enough protein in his diet. He taught her how to use hot then cold compresses to stimulate blood flow, and gave her a remedy for my upset stomach. This most remarkable man was not only available to his patients while he was dying, he was also working on exercises to help ease the strain of being bedridden for patients who were confined to their beds for long periods of time.

A couple of weeks after the doctor had cured my stomach ache, he died. His funeral was held in a beautiful rose garden behind the church. The Seventh Dayers sang hymns of joy and deliverance. They gave thanks to the Lord for transporting the soul of their brother to heaven where he would eventually join his previously departed family members, and be happy in the presence of the Lord forever. No one cried. They all seemed peaceful and very glad that their beloved doctor would at last go to his spiritual home. I found my Italian mother sobbing in the corner of the garden, her tears falling on a yellow rose bush. Tears that foreshadowed those she would shed when Peter died an untimely death a few years later.

One day seemed to drift into the next, one adventure into another. No one wore a watch and we didn't have a calendar. Months passed. Some days were very hot, and on others we kept our potbelly stove going all day long. I learned how to read. My mother sang a lot. Michael was really happy and played with me every day. Peter just kept the bus moving from one adventure to the next.

A year and a half after it had begun, our travels on the bus ended. Michael eventually finished school and became a nurse, my mother and I immigrated to Canada, and Peter died.

CANADA
I am five

"I know he's only five," my mother explained to the principal for the second time, "but he's reading on the third grade level."

"Absolutely not, Mrs. Dehr," countered the principal, " he will not go into first grade, he will go into kindergarten with his peer group. Now come with me please." My mother and I followed him out of his office and down a long, long hallway that was lined with lockers and strewn with sweaters and coats because winter had come early that year. Just before the hall made a sharp right turn, I saw an open door with a sign over it.

"E...X...I...T," I read aloud. " Exit, let's get out of here mom."

"Okay, first grade," conceded the principal. And so began my first day of school in Vancouver, British Columbia, Canada.

My mother and I had immigrated to Canada a year before. She had made the decision to leave the United States for several reasons: she was opposed to the war in Vietnam and swore that no government was going to give me a draft card on my eighteenth birthday, she was intrigued by this beautiful city and the soft strength of the Canadian people she had met, and she thought that kids grew up too fast in Los Angeles and hoped living in Vancouver would extend my childhood a little longer. We kind of felt like pioneers.

The woman at immigration told my mother that British

Columbia didn't need any more teachers, so when she filled out the immigration forms, my mom said she was a health food specialty baker. When the border official asked her what a health food specialty baker was, she replied, "Ha, you don't know, so you obviously don't have one!" He smiled at her and let us in.

To satisfy her immigration requirements, my mother had to open a bakery. And so, with the help of her friends Geri Larkin and Jaqui Manet, the Sunshine Bakery was born in our kitchen and we became landed immigrants.

Canada was good to us. My mother progressed from being a baker to the director of public relations for a major charity and then to owning her own publishing company. And I skipped kindergarten and had a pretty smooth childhood.

ZOE IS BORN
I am eight

Every morning during breakfast, my mother and I would discuss the dreams we had the night before. One morning she told me she dreamt she was a bird with straw in its beak, flying through the sky looking for a place to build a nest. She said she had dreamt that very same dream one year before I was born. One year later she gave birth to my sister Zoe.

Zoe wasn't such a bad kid. She giggled when I poked her. When she was old enough to be pushed around in a stroller, things became a bit more interesting. Someone had given my mother a bright pink collapsible stroller. Zoe and I went through that one and its next two replacements in a matter of weeks. Then, at a garage sale, my mom bought a homemade, rusted old stroller with an uncomfortable plastic seat. It was held together with yards of duct tape, and had really big wheels with ball bearings in them. The thing was indestructible. No matter how high the curb I ran Zoe off, it wouldn't collapse. One day my mom caught me flying down a very steep hill sitting in the stroller with Zoe on my lap. She ran after us screaming.

I remember how excited mom and I were when Zoe said her first word. It was "Or"— Thor — it was me. She said a couple more words a few days later, and two months after that she could almost say an entire sentence. It was fun listening to her pick up words and wondering what she would say next, until I realized she wasn't ever going to stop talking. Zoe would follow me around the house yelling

"Or, Or, Or, get me a cookie, it's on the uppest shelf." "Or, Or, Or, look, it's raining snow outside."

It didn't take long until she had enough words to ask me a million questions: "Where does God Live? What does God Eat? Does God have a toilet? Why is the sky so high? What's under all the dirt? Since we took a short cut to the store, can we take a long cut back home? Where is the West Pole?"

I had to laugh the day she saw two jugglers and called them "jugulars." One day I bounced a ball off the top of Zoe's head and she ran to mom yelling that I had hit her five-head. It took us a few minutes to figure out that the ball had hit her on the top of her head just above her forehead, and so she thought it must have been her five-head.

One sunny afternoon my mom packed a lunch and the three of us went for a picnic in Stanley Park, a beautiful park just fifteen minutes from home. After lunch, I played with Zoe. I pushed her on a swing and she laughed a lot, even when I tried to push her hard enough to make the swing go in an entire circle — but I couldn't push that hard. Next we played on the teeter-totter and I tried to flip her off, but her little legs had a good grip and she was laughing so hard and having such a good time that I stopped trying. My mom stood under a tree watching us with a look on her face that I couldn't identify because I had never seen it before.

The next week mom packed us into the car and we went to Langley, a town about an hour from our house, for a picnic. It took us a while to find a nice park with stuff for kids to play on, but we finally found one. After lunch, I taught Zoe how to crawl up a slide and slide down backward on her stomach. Mom watched us with that same look, but this time she had a smile on her face.

A week later mom borrowed some sleeping bags and a tent and we drove a few hours to Alice Lake to spend the weekend camping. We had a lot of fun that weekend. When we went on a hike, I ran ahead on the trail, hid behind a tree and jumped out at mom and Zoe and pretended I was a bear. In the hot afternoon, we swam in Alice Lake, a big lake with an old, extinct volcano towering above it. Mom put Zoe in a little round orange donut-like thing that floated, and we pushed her back and forth between us.

"Why is the lake cold over there and not over here?" Zoe asked me.

When I answered, "Because you're swimming where the fish pee," mom started to laugh and splashed me with water.

At night, my mom cooked over a Primus stove she said was trying to kill her, and we toasted marshmallows over a campfire on sticks I found in the woods. When we were in the tent, in our sleeping bags, mom told us stories about the bird with the straw in its beak and about how our grandmother, who had died shortly after Zoe was born, was watching us from heaven. Zoe and I fell asleep in the dark, dark quiet night.

The next morning, while Zoe and I helped mom load the camping gear into the car, I noticed my mom's strange look was gone, but her smile wasn't. "We're going to travel now," was all she said.

NEW YORK
Zoe is three and I am eleven

I remember coming home from school and finding my mother trying to make sense of a map. She had a horrible sense of direction and in order to use a map, the road she was on had to be pointing in a vertical direction. That meant that every time she made a turn she had to readjust the map. I think there is a correlation between people who have a poor sense of direction and people who hate maps. If somewhere there exists such a group of people, my mother would be their queen. I seldom saw her voluntarily hold a map, but when she did, I knew that our summer had been planned. No scout camp for us, no beach parties or long bike rides with friends—my mother had bigger fish to fry.

Our first excursion into the unknown was when my sister was three and I was eleven. Our mother decided that we should spend the summer in New York City. She told us that if we could survive that city, the entire world would be ours to explore. Within two hours of landing at LaGuardia Airport, my mother had us in a helicopter. "The city is so mammoth and there are just too many lines on this damn map," she said. "I thought we should get another perspective on it."

I sat in the front seat with the pilot and watched as the city disappeared under our feet. My mother and sister sat behind us. I didn't see how it happened, but somehow my sister dropped her little red doll out the window. It hung on the helicopter's struts for a while, and when we were above the Hudson River, between the shoreline and the Statue of Liberty, we watched it swirl down into the water.

"My doll's near that lady," yelled Zoe, "the one holding the ice cream cone."

My mother contended that having a mission was a wonderful way to explore a city. Our mission was to explore the big lady holding the ice cream cone, and then locate or duplicate Zoe's doll. We climbed to the top of the Statue of Liberty. Zoe gave out after about 23 steps, so my mother carried her the next 23. I dragged, pushed and carried her the rest of the way to the top. The view was great, but Zoe was upset that she couldn't find her red doll.

We spent many days going to dozens of stores all over New York City. Our search took us to Bloomingdales, Saks, FAO Schwartz and little shops in Harlem. We spent most of one day lost on the subways, but even that was an adventure. By the time Zoe found just the right little red doll replacement, we were in command of the city.

The only thing my mother feared was the night. She found a very small, inexpensive hotel room for us on the 34th floor of a building just opposite the Empire State Building. It must have been a nice hotel at one time because my mom raved about its art deco exterior. Once inside, you could tell that the hotel had fallen on hard times. Other than the very intricate design on the lobby floor, and some fancy woodwork on the check-in desk, the place was a dump. The lobby smelled from the stale cigarettes that overflowed the standing ashtray. Newspapers and dog-eared travel brochures covered an old wooden table, others joined cigarette butts, discarded cigarette packs and candy wrappers on the floor. The cigar-smoking clerk with missing teeth who checked us in smiled at my mother and asked her if her husband would be joining her. "Any day now," she answered, "after his next game. He's a 250-pound hockey goalie."

Our hotel room had two single beds with metal headboards, a dresser with a lamp on it, a hardback chair and a picture of the Empire State Building that had been nailed to the wall. This barren place became our home for the next few weeks, and by dusk the three of us were snugly inside eating a picnic dinner on the pushed-together beds, with the chair braced under the doorknob.

There was a terrible summer storm one night. While I was trying to convince Zoe that lightning came to take away little girls who didn't obey their brothers, a bolt hit the Empire State Building. It struck the lightning rod at the top of the building, and suddenly there was a flash and a shower of sparks accompanied by a peculiar smell my mom said was ozone. Our terrified mother made us sit out the rest of the storm in the middle of the bed with the bedding wrapped around us. Even though the nights kept us prisoners in our hotel room, and even though my mother's fear of lightning increased tenfold, she was triumphant, for we had survived New York City, and now the world was going to be ours to explore!

THAILAND
Zoe is four and I am twelve

We rode through the streets of Bangkok in open three-wheeled taxis that spewed carbon monoxide and made a loud noise that sounded like "tuc tuc tuc." That's why people called them tuc-tucs. As we drove from one gridlocked intersection to another, Thai women riding in other tuc-tucs would reach across and gently touch Zoe's face or hair, always avoiding the crown of her head where the God energy flowed. Some women gave her flowers and sweets, one presented her with a fried frog on a stick. Having been tutored by our mother on both the customs of other people and the plight of impoverished people in the third world, Zoe smiled gratefully at the frog lady and handed the impaled fried thing to me. Moments later the frog lady tuc-tuced away, and I awarded the frog to a little guy in the tuc-tuc behind her. Thailand is called the land of a million smiles, and I have proof of that because that's about how many people smiled at Zoe.

My mother pointed out that Bangkok is one of Asia's most cosmopolitan cities. It is crowded, polluted and very noisy, but when you venture into the palaces and Buddhist temples the six million people seem to disappear and it feels as if you are in old Siam. My mother took us to see the Reclining Buddha that is 46 meters long and 15 meters high, and has mother-of-pearl on the soles of its feet. We saw monks in saffron robes selling thin strips of gold leaf that you can press onto the body of the massive Buddha. My mother was right, the smell of incense and flowers and the sight of people at prayer did make this place seem timeless. The air, filled with hundreds of tiny flakes of gold, made me feel as if I were breathing magic.

Zoe spent her fourth birthday in Hua Hin, a beautiful beach resort that was our reward for a grueling five-hour train ride. On the train, we shared plank benches with a man carrying a box of chickens, a family with three crying babies, lots of people carrying bundles that were too heavy for them, two small goats and another frog lady. This time the pierced frog made Zoe cry. There was a sudden hush in the carriage. Even the three babies and the two goats stopped making that horrible why-am-I-in-a-train noise. The little foreign child was in distress. The women surrounded her, dried her tears, made humming clucking noises and plied her with sweets. I held onto the stick and while everyone's attention was on Zoe, I chucked the offending frog out the window. Now they would think that Zoe was crying because I had eaten her frog. I saw that "every child belongs to every woman, aren't women wonderful" look on my mother's face, and all I could think was, thank God they were out of frogs and we had finally reached Hua Hin.

Three days later my sister awakened completely covered in red spots. My mother quickly pulled the bedding off her feverish body to see if there were insects in her bed. Finding none, she wrapped Zoe in a sheet, yelled for me to gather the money belt and traveling documents and ran down the stairs and out the front door. "I need an English-speaking cab driver," she cried out. Three tuc-tucs nearly collided coming to her rescue. "Take me to an English-speaking doctor," she commanded. Because I had spent time locking the door of our room, I was a few feet behind her when she jumped into the cab, and had to run down the street to catch up with them.

After a quick examination, the doctor told my mother that Zoe had Dengue Fever, a mosquito-carried malady that was common in the tropics and subtropics, and had plagued the American troops in Vietnam. He told us that it would take several weeks for Zoe to recover from the malaria-like symptoms as she was so young, and Dengue Fever was a serious illness. He gave my mother a list of medicines that would help reduce Zoe's fever and make her more comfortable. No prescriptions are needed in Thailand, for all medicines are sold over the counter at the corner medical stores. His list was immediately rejected by my health-food-loving mother. That afternoon found us walking down a beach, my mother carrying Zoe, still wrapped in the bed sheet, me trailing behind. We were looking for someone to cure my sister.

Our search led us to an old woman sitting under a large palm leaf lean-to. Mom lay Zoe at her feet, clasped her hands in prayer and bowed her head. The woman poked at Zoe for a bit and disappeared down the beach. Mom told me to go swimming while she and Zoe waited for the woman to return. I swam and played in the warm turquoise water for about half an hour until I saw the old woman return to the lean-to. Mom and I watched as she spread something white and sticky on Zoe and then shake some greenish powder all over her. When she began to hum I went back into the water.

When the old woman was finished she again disappeared back down the beach. Zoe was sleeping comfortably in the shade of the lean-to, and my exhausted mother was just beginning to relax when something wrapped itself around my left leg, and I felt a searing pain. I ran out of the water, and when the Thai boys who had been swimming near me saw the streaks on my leg they called out "jellyfish, jellyfish," and quickly left that spot. The people nearby assured my frantic mother that the sting was not lethal, and that the long, dark tendril shapes on my leg would fade quicker if I stayed out of the sun for a few days. I made sure to spend as much time in the sun as I could. I thought the streaks were cool.

The old woman's white sticky stuff and green powder seem to have worked, because by that evening Zoe was symptom free, and just as much of a pest as she had been before she had become ill.

While traveling, we lived on a diet of fruit, cooked rice and vegetables. My mother was fanatic about all fruit being peeled, all vegetables being cooked and all dairy products being avoided. In Thailand we drank only bottled water, and she checked the caps religiously. We brushed our teeth with bottled water, when it was available, and hot tea when it was not. Ice was forbidden, bread and rice were encouraged.

One sweltering day, while eating rice and cooked vegetables in a small restaurant, Zoe begged mom for a crushed ice drink like the one the little girl at the neighboring table was having. Mom instructed me to trace the ice. I followed the waiter back into the kitchen, and when he went into the back alley I hid behind a pile of banana boxes. When I heard a chipping sound I peeked around the boxes and saw the waiter squatting on the ground in front of a very large block of ice, chipping it with a hammer and chisel. When he had enough slivers of ice, he scooped them off the very dirty ground and put them in a soft drink. I ran back to our table and vetoed the crushed ice drink. Zoe put up so much of a fuss that I had to promise to carry her piggyback to keep her quiet. But after that, I never again questioned my mother's fanatic attention to what we ate and drank.

The Khlongs

I find it difficult to write about a typical traveling day because my mother was propelled by such an enormous sense of adventure that every day was exciting. Take for example the day we were told to put on our best clothes and bring our jackets even though it was a blue sky day and treacherously hot. We rode across town on a crowded bus, and as we passed the very posh Oriental Hotel, my mom told us that we were going there. Two stops later we got off the bus and she hailed a cab to drive us seven blocks back to the hotel. The doorman opened the cab door for us and bowed to my mother. The mâitre d' found our name and ushered us to a table. To our surprise, my mother had made reservations for the brunch buffet.

From our table we could look down at the Khlongs, Thailand's three-hundred-year-old intricate system of canals and waterways. We could see men in long boats buying and selling their wares. Some boats were filled with flowers, and others were laden with produce. It was a floating supermarket.

Our waiter appeared at our table and told us that the sumptuous buffet was prepared with the tourist's delicate stomach in mind. He assured us that the lettuce had even been washed in bottled water.

For the first time in six weeks Zoe and I were able to eat and drink anything we wanted. Zoe headed for a crushed ice drink, and I for a milkshake. When we had finished eating more than we thought we could ever consume, my mother caught our waiter's eye, put a tip on the table and began stuffing our jacket pockets with fruit. The waiter nodded and smiled, and handed me a small bag of candies when we left.

Our next stop was, of course, the Khlongs. Many boats were for hire, and as we neared the shore people called to us to choose theirs. Mom went directly to a boat that was rowed by a pregnant woman. We floated around the vendors' boats for a while, and then the woman steered us further down the river. After a while we came to a kind of town where some people lived on houseboats and others in dwellings that were held up by poles and sticks and seemed to be half in the water and half on the ground. We saw small children tethered to boats by cords around their feet, and older children playing and swimming in polluted water in which people dumped garbage and human waste. My mom waved to a group of children, and when they swam up to our boat Zoe and I gave them the fruit in our jacket pockets and the candy in the bag. If my mother's aim was to make Zoe and me aware of the poor people in the world, she succeeded, for the image of those children swimming in polluted water with fresh apples in their hands and big smiles on their faces will stay with me for the rest of my life.

The Street of Jewels

My mother would have been a wonderful spy, for having a mission both motivated and consumed her. Christie Moon was her childhood friend. Our mission: to buy Christie Moon a moonstone. Bangkok is known for its precious gemstones, and the small stores on the Street of Jewels is where they are sold. The displays are few, and the quiet men who stand in the corners of the shops and closely watch the customers are many. When a customer enters a shop and asks the jeweler for a certain kind of stone, a black velvet cloth is placed on the counter before him, and the jeweler spills a bag of the stones onto the cloth. The jeweler then uses long tongs to show the customer the particular qualities of each stone. The customer does

34

not touch the merchandise until the jeweler removes all but one or two of the stones and hands him the tongs. Jewelers on the Street of Jewels arc often too busy to pay much attention to people who wish to buy a single semi-precious moonstone.

We watched people of many nationalities leave the shops with thousands of dollars in precious stones before we took our turn. We told the man behind the counter that we wanted to view some moonstones. He politely suggested that if we didn't like faceted stones he had some emeralds that were particularly nice. Wc politely, and a bit apologetically, asked again for moonstones. He spread the black velvet cloth before us and emptied a bag that must have contained fifty stones. The fiery brilliance beneath their milky opalescence shimmered before us.

"How do we know which are the good stones?" asked my mother. I think that if it hadn't been for Zoe, who looked particularly cute with her eyes and her mouth wide open, the jeweler would have packed up his rocks at that point, but something about a little foreign child seems to win the hearts of the Thai people. He told us that the shape was important and pointed out which were the best shapes. We thanked him politely and left.

The proprietor of the next shop was impressed by our knowledge of moonstone shapes and told us how to measure the brilliance of each stone. We went from shop to shop, learning a little more in each one. By midday we considered ourselves experts, and a short while later we found the perfect moonstone for Christie Moon!

Monsoons

Sheets of rain hurt our skin when they hit, and saturated our clothing within seconds. My job was to grab Zoe and follow my mother to the nearest shelter. Once we found a doorway, and mom and I pushed Zoe against the door and formed a barrier with our bodies to protect her from the rain. Another time, at a marketplace, we hid under a table. I slid Zoe on top of a cage filled with chickens and mom and I cuddled around her. The chickens pecked at Zoe through the wire and she yelled a little, but she stayed a lot dryer than we did.

The Night Market

We seldom ventured out at night, but one night in northern Thailand, I was finally able to convince my mother to go to a well-known night market just a few blocks from our hotel. When we left our room that night I held Zoe's hand tightly. I was feeling very responsible because my mother had put our passports, traveling papers and all the cash we had in a canvas pouch and asked me to wear it under my shirt. She thought no crook would ever look there because an adult would never entrust a child with all that responsibility.

We could hear music and laughter about a block before we reached the market. The smell of cooked pork and heavy spices hung in the night air. Colorful makeshift stalls had been set up on the sidewalks and people ambled up and down the street. Everyone seemed to know everyone else, and they called to each other from stall to stall. We were probably the only tourists there. When women saw Zoe they would leave their stalls, run up to her and touch her face. Many of them gave her trinkets and sweets. Everyone wanted a smile from the little foreign child.

My mother was just about to buy me a great shirt with a dragon on it when she saw ten beggars sitting a few feet from each other, each with a bowl in front of them, and each with the same kind of malformed limbs. Some had little fish-like fingers sticking out where their arms should have been, others had feet-like things extending a few inches from their torsos, and one had both arms and legs missing. They were all the same age. My mother went from stall to stall asking about the beggars. She wanted to know why they had the same kind of deformities and why they were all the same age. Everyone knew, but no one could speak enough English to tell her. Finally, a young man who had been walking behind us for a while put his hand on my mother's arm. "Thalidomide," he said, "they sold the drug to us when it was banned in the States." All of their mothers had taken Thalidomide to prevent morning sickness, and their children had been born deformed. My mother moaned, and involuntarily her hands rushed to her chest. A moment later, her hands rushed to my chest.

She ripped the canvas pouch away from me and gave every cent in it to the old Thalidomide children.

Geckos

Geckos are little green lizards that eat bugs and live in your room. My mother had great respect for anything that ate bugs, so Zoe and I were commanded to try to love them. The geckos weren't easy to love because in the night they would scamper up the walls and across the ceiling in an effort to reach the bare light bulb that attracted flies, moths and a variety of other insects. Gulping down a bug caused the geckos to throw their little green heads back thereby loosing their grip on the ceiling and falling onto the ground. I hated them. For some reason they continued to cross the ceiling after the bug-attracting light was out, and we could hear them making plopping sounds as they hit the floor. After one fell on my head when I was asleep, I begged my mom to take us to a place were there weren't any geckos.

The next day we packed our canvas bag and headed for the train station. We were heading south to Malaysia because my mother had heard that the beaches were unspoiled by tourists, and there were fewer geckos. After standing in line for a long time, then dealing with a ticket clerk who wanted a tip but didn't know how to ask for it in English, my mother emerged with three tickets in her hand. Our soon-departing train was at the far end of the platform. It would be tight, but we had to make it because the clerk, who had not received a tip, had stamped our tickets non-refundable. To complicate matters, Zoe, who had stayed awake late into the night because she was afraid a gecko would fall on her, had fallen into a dead sleep. Mom picked her up and dashed down the platform leaving me to struggle with my pack and our canvas bag. We made it with seconds to spare, but my mother, three feet from the boarding steps, stood rooted to the spot. "We're not getting on that train," she said. When I asked her why, she repeated, "We're just not getting on that train."

Back at the gecko hotel my mother told me that if I ever have an odd feeling about a moving vehicle, I should never get into it, no matter what. Due to her "odd feeling," we abandoned the pristine

37

beaches of Malaysia, slept that night with the sheet over our heads to protect us from the falling geckos, and the next day took a bus north to Chiang Mai. Several weeks later we heard the train we would have been on had been waylaid along a deserted stretch and all the passengers had been robbed.

Chiang Mai

In Chiang Mai, we found a guesthouse that was mercifully free of geckos. The two-storey structure that contained the sleeping rooms was built around a central courtyard where there were several tables and benches, and a three-foot concrete shrine with offerings set before it shaded by graceful coconut palm trees. For a few baht more we could join the owner and his family in the courtyard for dinner. It was a deal, and many of the guests met every night for excellent Thai cuisine.

The bathroom was in a small building a few feet behind the sleeping rooms. There were four toilets. Each consisted of two bricks, a hole, a bucket of water and a tin can. You had to stand on the bricks, squat, go to the bathroom and then scoop water out of the bucket with the tin can and pour it down the hole. The bathroom was easier for me to use than it was for my mom, but it was impossible for Zoe because she was afraid of the hole, and she would scream every time we took her there. The only way the kid would pee was for mom to hold her under her arms, and for me to hold her feet, and we would kind of swing her over the hole while she screamed.

One evening, two young Frenchmen watched my mother as she placed a chunk of something white on a mirror, took out a razor blade and chopped it into powder. She then placed the powder in a spoon and added a bit of honey to it. Their intrigue turned to horror when my mom coaxed Zoe to swallow it. "Mon Dieu, what are you feeding zat leetle girl child," they cried. They were greatly relieved when my mother told them it wasn't cocaine, it was a malaria pill.

We spent the next couple of evenings comparing notes with Jacques and François, and swapping stories about the sights we had seen and the people we had met that day. They told us about the

Chiang Mai nightlife, the clubs and the bars, and we told them about the elephants we had seen in the jungle and the school room that didn't have enough books. Their room was directly above ours, and in the early morning hours, we could hear them come in and stumble up the steps laughing and singing French songs.

Lightning

I was sound asleep when my mother awakened me. "Quickly Thor," she said, " a bolt of lightning came through the ceiling and landed at the foot of my bed. We've got to get out of here. Hurry, Thor, help me with Zoe!"

Moments later Zoe and I were standing in the courtyard in our pajamas with our mother, who was so upset she was breathing hard and her hands were shaking. "What bolt of lightning?" I asked her. It was only then that she realized she had been asleep and had dreamed the lightening bolt. Zoe sat on her lap and I brought her a canteen of water and a glass. The three of us sat in the courtyard for about ten minutes until our mother had calmed down enough to go back to bed.

As we were heading back to our room, we heard a scream from the room above ours. My mother told me to stay in the courtyard with Zoe and not to move under any circumstances, and then she ran up the stairs.

When she reached the door of the Frenchmen's room she saw François vomiting into a bucket. Jacques was dead. After a night of drugs and alcohol he had aspirated in his sleep. Zoe and I quietly crept up the stairs, stood at the door and watched our mother frantically search for Jacques' pulse. When she saw us, she shouted at me to get Zoe out of the room immediately, to awaken the owner and then go back to our room and not let go of Zoe's hand until she returned.

The owner awakened the other guests and asked them to gather in the courtyard. When we were assembled he told us that he would call the police in half an hour, and in that time we were to search our rooms thoroughly for any signs of drugs. When one of the guests insisted he didn't use drugs, the owner told him to search his room in case the previous guest had left even a marijuana seed behind. He told us the Thai police had no sympathy for foreigners who overdosed on drugs. Since the death was drug related, there was no telling what they would do when they arrived.

When the guests were reassembled in the courtyard, the owner told François to gather his things and take a taxi to the address on the piece of paper he handed him. He was to leave the city at dawn and never return. My mother gave François some money and tried to comfort him. He left, and the police were called.

Two policemen came in a truck, interrogated the owner and asked him which of the guests had known, or had ever spoken with the dead person. I told Zoe that if she said anything I would put a gecko in her bed. When no one responded, the police marched up the stairs. My mom was so busy trying to explain what had happened to Zoe in a way that would neither frighten nor mark her for life that she didn't see me follow the policemen.

I watched from the doorway of the neighboring room as they removed Jacques' body. Each policeman took one of his legs and pulled him down the stairs — his head bouncing and thudding on each step. When they reached the bottom of the stairs, the policemen dragged him through the courtyard and threw him into the back of their truck.

After the truck left, I ran around the guesthouse and walked into the courtyard as if I had been in the bathroom. Zoe had fallen asleep in mom's arms so, fortunately, had not witnessed the removal of the body. My mother, thinking I had been in the bathroom, was happy that I had not witnessed it either. The two Frenchmen were gone, one was in hiding, the other dead. My mother began to cry as did several of the other women. The Thai guests placed offerings before the shrine and prayed for the spirit of the dead man. It was very quiet. Then suddenly we heard a loud crashing sound — a coconut had fallen on the shrine. The Thai people fell to their knees. They told us, "the spirit of the dead boy is very angry."

The next day my mother told us to put our bathing suits on under our best clothes. We walked into the Chiang Mai Hilton, which was holding a convention for North American and European cardiovascular surgeons. My mom told the man at the desk to inform Dr. Jonathan Peters, when he checked in, that his family would be waiting for him in the pool area. Zoe and I spent the rest of the day playing in the pool while our mother sat in a deck chair, her face shaded by a newly acquired straw hat that masked the tears that ran down her cheeks. The lightning bolt that she had dreamt had pierced the soul of the French boy sleeping in the room above us, and had landed at the foot of her bed.

The last week we spent in Thailand lacked the magic of the previous ones. My mom seemed sad and tired and we spent most of the time on the beach—mom reading and me trying to guard Zoe from the jellyfish. As we were packing to return home, I noticed mom had left a guidebook and map of China on the bed. I guessed we were going there next summer.

CHINA
Zoe is five and I am thirteen.

A year and a half before I was born, my mother was in a severe car crash. She broke 23 bones and had her spleen removed. Her doctors told her that it would be far too risky for her to have children. But, both times she dreamt of the bird with the straw in its beak, she gave thanks and put her life on the line, first giving birth to me and then to my sister. Had she been able to bear children more easily, she would have birthed a multitude, but since she could not, children came to her.

Zoe and I shared our home and our mother's love with the children who found her. First, Namchi and Kaima, whom she loved as deeply as she loved Zoe and me, and who became sisters to both of us. Then there were Alex, Keith and Winston who became our brothers, and Steve, Brie, Ken and Tabatha, Sebastien, Shea, Natasha, Sarah Rose and Sky. My mother befriended street kids, who passed through our home. Dinner was served to whomever was there and we all joined in the clean-up. She sheltered runaway women, no questions asked, and when she first came to Canada, her home was a stop on the underground railroad for Vietnam draft dodgers. The phone rang at all hours, and midnight counseling sessions were many. For the months of the school year, we shared our mother's time, energy and affection with others. During the summer months she was ours.

One June, the spleenectomy scar on my mother's abdomen herniated and had to be repaired. Before she left the hospital, the doctor told her she should not lift anything heavier than a teacup for the next month. We left for China three days later.

Hong Kong

We arrived in Hong Kong hot, exhausted and badly in need of sleep. My mom decided the quickest way to find an inexpensive and safe hotel was to ask a policeman to recommend one. The first policeman we found told us to go down a side street until we reached a crowded tunnel that would lead us to an inside mall. He said we would find a door marked "hotel" inside the mall. We followed his directions.

Among the stalls and small shops that lined the mall were quiet looking doors with no markings. The ceiling of the mall was completely obscured by interlacing wires and cables. Dangling extension cords, attached to extension cords, attached to extension cords fed electricity to the shops and stalls below. Eventually, we came upon a door simply marked "Hotel". It was just in time as Zoe needed to go to the bathroom. The man at the check-in desk took a night's rent in advance and handed my mother two keys—one to the room, the other to the bathroom down the hall.

Our room was on the fifth floor. There was no elevator. The minute we opened the door we were nearly overcome by the smell of camphor. As she did in every "inexpensive" hotel room, my mother crept quietly to the bed, grabbed the bedding and pulled it back with one swift move. The three of us then examined the mattress to see if anything scurried for cover. Having declared the small bed bug free, mom took Zoe to the bathroom down the hall and I collected the source of the camphor smell—mothballs.

A few minutes later, mom and Zoe returned with tales of a bathroom with no toilet seats or wastebasket, and a machine over the sink that you had to put money in to get hot water. When I showed mom the 23 mothballs I had found in the room, she gasped, "Throw them out the window immediately, and leave the window open to air out the room."

When I threw the mothballs out the screenless window the

rancid odor of garbage replaced the smell of camphor. The courtyard below, flanked on four sides by the five-storey building, was filled with trash up to the second floor. Evidently we hadn't been the only guests to pitch stuff out the window.

That night, as the three of us attempted to sleep in the single bed, our noisy neighbors slammed doors and threw bottles out the windows. And all night long they laughed and moaned and their beds made squeaking, thumping sounds — we had rented a room in a brothel.

Jet lag so distorted our sense of time that five-year-old Zoe and I hardly noticed that we arrived before the merchants at Hong Kong's early morning market. As people set up their tables and my mother carried on about the anthropological significance of the marketplace for all aboriginal peoples, Zoe and I wandered up and down between the stalls and saw the most amazing array of edibles. There were buckets of eels, snakes, fish and frogs, and cages of kittens. But what interested me the most were the items I could not identify. There were fruits with spikes sticking out of them, dark red and black eggs and things that looked like a cross between insects and something larger. I tried to keep Zoe from getting in people's way, but when I wasn't looking, someone slapped her on the head with a plastic bag of decapitated and pealed frogs that were in death spasms, and she began to cry.

Zoe would not be mollified by the lychee fruit mom had bought from one of the vendors, so we headed for the nearest restaurant. It was easy to order because the menu was pictorial. We pointed to the toast and orange juice and asked for three servings. The waiter returned with egg sandwiches and tea and we enjoyed a good breakfast.

Two days before we were to leave Hong Kong and travel to Mainland China, we were caught by the beginning of a typhoon. We had ducked into an underground shopping center to get out of what we thought was just a bad storm. We were only three blocks from our hotel but the gusting winds frightened my mother, and she was hesitant to leave the shelter of the shopping center. I told her we should make a run for it because they were boarding up the place, and it looked as if the wind was getting worse rather than better. We each held one of Zoe's hands and tried to run across the street when a gust of wind caused Zoe to become airborne. When she fell to the ground, we grabbed her under her arms and barely made it to the other side. The wind slammed us hard against the buildings and it took us a quite a while to walk to the end of that block. We had one more intersection and another block to go before we would be safe in our hotel. It seemed so very far away. The wind had claimed my mother's scarf and the bag of food I carried in my non-Zoe-clutching hand. The rain was coming down so hard we couldn't see very far, and we were so wet we felt as if we had fallen into a swimming pool. We waited at the corner until the next big gust came and went, and then we made a dash for it. I could tell mom was afraid, and it was hard for me to keep being brave, but Zoe was having a great time. As we ran and stumbled across the streets holding her under her arms, she pulled up her legs, curled into a ball and laughed all the way. The last block was a bit easier than the one before as we discovered that if we crouched down and moved in a clump, like a low slung insect with six legs, we could go faster. After we reached the safety of our hotel, the typhoon ripped the sign off the building, shattering it at the entrance we had come through twenty minutes before.

Mainland China

Mainland China was incredibly interesting because of its massive numbers of people and how quickly change took place. The Great Hall of the People had a meeting room that held 10,000 people, a banquet room that served 10,000 people, 300 very large rooms and a massive museum. It took only ten months to build.

We traveled in a small bus with fifteen other people, one of whom was a Canadian woman named Judy Rother. At last, our mother had someone with whom to discuss anthropological significances, and they became close friends. Most of the other people on the bus were Chinese. Zoe began learning Chinese words and soon became everyone's darling little child. We saw such wonders: monasteries, carved Buddhas, clay Buddhas, gold Buddhas, pagodas, silk and jade factories and weavings that were made with the blind stitch — a stitch so small that the weavers who used it lost their sight, and finally the stitch was banned.

We traveled north where people had never seen Western children and were very curious about us. Everyone wanted to touch Zoe, and once she was so mobbed that even though mom and I had a death grip on her hands, we couldn't see her. People thought of me as an oddity because I was obviously a teenager and yet much taller than they were. They would come right up to me, stand on their tiptoes and look into my blue eyes. That always made me smile, and then when they saw my braces they would scream and jump back. Everywhere we were on display.

The summer we spent in China was unusually hot. I took a picture of Zoe lying on my mom's lap. It was so hot that their faces were wet and their clothes clung to their bodies so that they looked like a sculpted wax candle that was melting. To our credit, my sister and I never complained about the weather. My mother told everyone we were fantastic travelers, and even Zoe, at such a young age, realized that was a reputation she wanted to keep.

When we came to the great Yangtze River, my mother dipped her hands into its waters and vowed to take her children to its sister rivers, the Amazon and the Nile. Zoe and I exchanged glances that confirmed we both understood our mother was distinctly peculiar and our travels had just begun.

One of the many hotels in which we stayed stands out in my mind. It was designed by Australians and there were koala bears and kangaroos on the curtains. The lobby, stairs and halls were covered in a plush red carpet with little pieces of straw sticking out of it because the janitors swept the carpet with handmade straw brooms. Our room was fine with the exception of the centipede in the very small bathtub and the bats that would fly in when we opened our window at night. I prayed the bats would consume the centipede.

My mother always avoided the elevators and insisted we take the stairs in countries in which technology was unreliable. That morning she elected to take the elevator because, due to her operation,

I had to carry both our canvas bag and my pack and it was already sweltering. When we entered the elevator, the surprised Chinese janitor descending from the floor above ours, his eyes more frightened than curious, quickly scampered to the back of the elevator. The door closed, we descended for a couple of floors, and then we stopped mid-floor. We pushed all the buttons, and nothing happened. I finally found a strange knob that when twisted sounded a faint alarm — at least that piece of technology worked. My mother instructed us to remain calm and conserve oxygen, and sat down on our canvas bag with Zoe on her lap. The Chinese man, on the verge of hysteria, trembled in the corner. "Go speak to him in Chinese," my mother whispered to Zoe, and so my brave little sister emptied her vocabulary onto the cringing man.

"My name is Zoe." "This is a pretty dress." "Thank you for the rice." "Where is the bathroom?" It didn't help at all. Now the man, wide-eyed with fear, was almost in tears.

Things were getting intense in that little box, and I made things worse when I suggested that it would probably take a while to get someone from Australia to fix the elevator. "Do something Thor," said my mother, so I banged on the door with my fists and started yelling, causing the Chinese man to break out in a sweat. At last the elevator lurched, and a dozen hands pried open the door. We climbed out, leaving our fellow passenger with a tale to tell, and just made the bus to Wuxi.

The main industry in Wuxi is the manufacture of silk. Experienced hands pluck cocoons from mulberry trees, dip each cocoon into boiling water for only a few seconds, skillfully find the end of the silk thread, then spool, dye, and weave the silk into scarves, ties and garments. We were fascinated by the process, and the factory workers were fascinated by us. Zoe delighted the women with her Chinese phrases and added more words to her vocabulary.

Just as we were about to leave, the factory manager presented us with a small dish of round candies that were sprinkled with crystallized sugar. Zoe, starving for sweets, gobbled hers down immediately. I let mine melt in my mouth. In fact, they were melting when my mom asked what the candies were made of and received the reply, "silk worms."

A Bus Ride

The memory of the silk worms in my mouth was just beginning to fade when we arrived in Shanghai. We stayed in the Park Hotel, famous because Chairman Mao stayed there when he was in Shanghai. From our hotel window on the thirteenth floor, we could see hundreds of people practicing Tai Chi in the neighboring park. As we walked through the park amid the shifting statues we were impressed by the skill of the very young and the very old.

One stifling night my mother decided we should walk to the shore of the river where she thought it had to be cooler. I was hesitant to venture into the Shanghai night, but she insisted the river couldn't be that far away as it was only an inch away on the map. With trepidation we took the elevator — the stairwells were impassable as they were used to store furniture.

There were few cars on the streets, and people had fled the sweltering confines of their homes to sit on crates and boxes under lampposts that were located a block apart. When we stopped at a lamppost to read our map, Zoe was swarmed by curious women. When I put her on my shoulders, we became even more of a curiosity and many, many people followed us. After a while, the heat began to get to me and Zoe began to squirm around on my shoulders in an effort to fall asleep with her head on my head.

At last we came to the shore, but it was so packed with people we couldn't get anywhere near it. When we stopped, we were surrounded by a very large crowd numbering in the hundreds, and we were unable to move in any direction. For the first time in my life I saw panic in my mother's eyes. We were surrounded, but even if we could have moved she had no idea where the hotel was, we didn't speak the language, and on top of that we were in Shanghai. Just then the crowd parted and pushed a young man toward us. He spoke English

China
Roma and Zoe
melting at
40 degrees Centigrade,
104 degrees Fahrenheit

U.S.S.R.
It was against the law to
photograph the military,.
To win a bet, Roma had to
bribe the officer in charge.

U.S.S.R.
Zoe sitting on a proletarian statue. Photograph taken at
5 A.M. to avoid the police.

Australia
My mother fell in love
with this desolate land.

Australia
Thor feeding an emu just prior to the
emu slamming him in the stomach
with its head.

Australia
Thor, Roma and Zoe standing behind the camel that
minutes later ran away into the outback with Zoe.

Australia
Zoe with a baby kangaroo called a joey.

Australia
Zoe and Thor standing next to a
giant termite mound.

Africa
Roma, Zoe and Nicholas, the guide
who took us into the bush.

Africa
Zoe playing with Massai children

Africa
Zoe with a playmate in Mombassa

Peru
*Thor, Zoe and Roma hiking into
the mountains above Machu
Picchu.*

Peru
*Thor, Zoe and Roma resting after
a long trek into the Amazon rainforest.*

Peru
Thor standing on top of Huayna Picchu.

Peru
Zoe and a llama smiling for the camera.

The Galapagos Islands
Zoe taking a photograph of a giant tortoise,
and so giving us a glimpse of her future.

that he had learned in school, and by talking with us he became an instant celebrity. People shouted questions at him and he asked us how old Zoe and I were, where we had come from, and where our father was. The people closest to us squatted down so that those behind could see and hear us. They seemed to have an infinite number of questions, and we enjoyed watching their reactions to our answers. When we told them we liked Chinese food they clapped, when we told them we were traveling without a father they shook their heads in wonder.

The crowd seemed to sway to the left when the young man pointed in that direction and called out "bus." "Busssss, busssss, busssss," chanted the crowd. Hands pressed us toward the bus, and when we got there, mom showed the bus driver the Park Hotel's card. When he nodded, mom and I squeezed aboard, and the crowd passed Zoe to us through a window. The driver called out to the passengers and we were politely shoved to the long seat at the back of the bus. Every time we came to a stop, some people got off the bus, and as others got on the driver whispered to them and they came to the back to look at us. The men giggled at me, and the women lightly touched Zoe's face and hair. Finally, we realized the driver had turned the bus into a moving museum and we were on exhibit. Hours later, hotter and more tired than we had been when we left, we were deposited at the door of our hotel, and all the passengers and the bus driver applauded as we got out.

The next morning, after leaving the airline terminal and crossing the hot tarmac to the boarding stairs of a plane going to Beijing, my mother realized that she had lost one of our three boarding passes. That meant we would miss this plane and have to stay in the airport for a long time while they checked and rechecked our passport, traveling papers and visitor's status. When we reached the top of the boarding ramp the steward asked for our boarding passes. Mom sort of dropped, sort of threw, the two we had into the wind of the propeller. As small pieces of the boarding passes fluttered across the field and the steward began to panic, we ran into the plane. Mom felt sorry for the steward because he would be blamed for the missing boarding passes, but she figured that he lived there and could afford to stay, while we needed to go to Beijing.

That night, in another Australian built and decorated hotel, we were treated to a variety show. Men played ancient instruments, women danced, young girls sang, and then more people played instruments, danced and sang. Zoe and I left when the entire cast came on stage to sing "Oh Susanna" in Chinese. My mom was long gone before that. She was in our room planning how to gain access to a hospital where access to visitors was restricted unless they were very ill.

The Hospital

By dangling Zoe in front of the head nurse, we were allowed entrance to a large hospital. We were given free reign of the place, with the exception of the operating rooms and the third floor where the women and children were being treated. Our first stop was the pharmacy, which dispensed both western and traditional medicine. We photographed great jars of leeches and eels, stacks of shark's fins, various tusks and mushrooms and herbs lining the walls. Busy pharmacists, using hand-held scales, weighed mixtures of exotic textures and colors, wrapped them in squares of paper and dispensed them to the never-ending line of patients. Sixty doctors and 100 nurses ministered to thousands of patients a day.

Behind the pharmacy and down a narrow hall, we came upon a large room with open skylights. The walls held three tiers of platforms upon which patients lay. On the floor were stools upon which other patients sat. Doctors and nurses circulated through the room inserting acupuncture needles to relieve pain. To draw toxins out of a body, the insides of jars that had been swabbed with alcohol were set on fire to heat them. Then the jars were placed on a person's flesh to draw it up into the vacuum the heat created. The patients sitting on stools were being treated with long acupuncture needles that had an incense-like substance on them that when lighted would fill the air with smoke and heat the needles to stimulate the acupuncture points.

A very old man sat on a stool with two long, smoking needles extending from his shoulders. His chest was bare and his robe hung from his waist in Da Vinci-like folds. The skylight back-lit his figure so that the smoke from the needles sparkled as it encircled his shoulders, neck and head. Spotting a *National Geographic* cover photo within her reach, my mother whipped out her camera and dropped to her knees before the ancient man. Her subject was silent, his gaze downward and steady, an aura of ancient wisdom permeating his visage. My mother positioned herself so he was looking directly into her lens. She focused her camera with care, and as the smoke completed a perfect ring above his head, she looked at his unmoving eyes. They said "No." Here within her reach was the photograph of a lifetime. Here also was a man whose privacy had been invaded at a time when he was vulnerable and ill, and through his eyes he had said "No." My mother, ever championing the rights of aboriginal people and opposed to western culture imposing its values upon them, looked directly into the man's eyes, pushed the release and took the photograph.

We kept careful records of the photographs we took. My mother had bracketed the picture of the ancient man to ensure proper exposure and had carefully marked the numbers nine, ten and eleven on the tenth roll of the twenty rolls of film we had taken. Weeks later, in the comfort of our living room, we viewed the slides of our trip. My mother was somehow less surprised than we were when every photograph we had taken was intact with the exception of the entire 10th roll. The ancient man had not let my mother take his picture.

Everywhere we went, the woman with the tall son with blue eyes and a metal mouth and the darling little foreign child were honored guests. When mom bought us second-class tickets on a boat down a river near Hangchow, a steward was sent to escort us to first class. The minute he left, mom dragged us back down the stairs to second class. All eyes were constantly on Zoe. Even though she had mastered chopsticks at an early age, mom had brought a fork for her to use at night when she was tired. It never failed, as soon as Zoe began to use the fork, the women servers would gather around her and remark, "oh look how well she uses a fork, and she's only a child."

For the past ten years, the provincial government had asked every one of the four million people who lived in Nanking to plant a tree every spring. Ten years later there were forty million trees in that city, there were trees everywhere, and my mother seemed to be allergic to all of them.

Perhaps it was the trees in Nanking, or the heat, or the pressure of propelling Zoe and me through the throngs of curious Chinese people that caused my mother to fall ill in Guilin. While Zoe and I enjoyed this mystic city, mom traveled from public toilet to public toilet returning with one horror story after another. The land where Guilin had been built had at one time been under the sea. When we first saw it, the tall thin mountains that stood apart from each other were bathed in an early morning haze, making it seem as if we were mysteriously underwater.

"I pooped black, I'm going to die!" cried my mother as she exited from a public toilet, toilet paper clutched to her breast. I calmly reminded her that she had taken a charcoal tablet that morning in an effort to absorb excess stomach acids. "Oh right. Thank God," she moaned and ran back into the public toilet.

China was a country of massive numbers. We saw the Nanjing Yangtze River Bridge, a four-mile bridge that was made with one million tons of steel and eleven million tons of concrete, and took 5,000 workers to build. We saw city walls that were twelve meters thick. The Dr. Sun Yat-Sen Mausoleum had 400 stairs. The Ming tomb had 36 concubines buried alive in it. The Forbidden City had walls 33 feet high, a moat 120 feet wide and grounds fifteen layers of bricks thick so no one could tunnel under them. Some stones weighed 250 tons and had been pulled 100 miles before they were fit into place. The Forbidden City had 9,999 rooms. Zoe, however, was much more intrigued by the young children who had slits in their panties so they could squat and pee and not wet their clothing.

The Great Wall
A smelly, overcrowded, sweltering bus jammed with tourists from all over the world drove us within 30 feet of the Great Wall. The minute we got off the bus and my mother saw the wall, tears filled her eyes. "Memorize this Thor, memorize this Zoe," she said,

"This is the most powerful engineering feat in the whole world. The Great Wall is a symbol of centuries of Chinese strength and power. If we were standing on the moon, we could see the Great Wall!"

The Great Wall of China is the only human-made thing that can be seen from outer space. Construction on the wall began in the seventh century B.C., and it was built and rebuilt over hundreds of years. It is about 3,800 miles in length, 15 feet wide, 24 feet tall, and 16 to 27 feet high. The Great Wall stretches from the mountains of Korea to the Gobi Desert. It is in every sense of the word—great!

We spent the day climbing around on the wall. My mother took pictures while I kept Zoe from falling to her death at least a dozen times. Mom told us that the ancient Chinese set fires of straw in the towers to let the soldiers know how many invaders were coming. One fire meant about 500, two fires meant 3,000 and so on. I agreed with mom that the Great Wall was magical because after hiking on it for a few hours we could easily imagine hordes of Mongols attacking from the west.

Someone told us that the bodies of the dead workers were buried in the wall, but I told them that I didn't think so because bodies are organic and when they rotted they would have weakened the wall. However, I did wonder what happened to the millions of people who lived and died building this wall. We bought Zoe a pink shirt that read "I climbed the Great Wall" in Chinese characters.

When my mother was a child, the United States did not recognize China because it was a communist country. She told me when she asked her elementary school teachers about China they tried to coax her into becoming interested in another country. One of her teachers even told her it was not a good idea to think about China too much. By the time she was twelve she had decided that someday she would visit that country.

My mother told us she wanted us to look at this fascinating country that was so burdened by its enormous population and draw our own political conclusions about it. She said that it was important for us to understand other systems of government for two reasons. First, because we would understand our own system of government better and appreciate it more, and second, because we were going to the Soviet Union next year.

THE TRANS-SIBERIAN RAILROAD
Zoe is seven and I am fifteen

We traveled with an old canvas suitcase that was divided into three compartments by two heavy-duty zippers. The middle compartment was for my mother's things, the first aid kit and a roll of duct tape. The two other compartments were for Zoe and me: seven underpants, a change of pants, four shirts, one bathing suit, seven pairs of socks, a toothbrush and a flashlight each. The list never varied. I carried a backpack filled with books that would be read on the trip, given away and replaced by souvenirs. We traveled light.

Besides the adventure of crossing Siberia, I think viewing the Rembrandt in the Hermitage at the end of the trip was what motivated my mother to risk life and limb on the Trans-Siberian Railroad. The trip began with a very long flight to Tokyo, and a boat ride that would take us north across the Sea of Japan to Vladivostok, where we would board the train.

The Sea of Japan

We were met at the dock by a group of Australians with whom we would be traveling. They had been informed that a woman with a seven-year-old daughter and a fifteen-year-old son would be joining them, and they weren't looking forward to it. However, they greeted us cordially, "Hey Lydee, let us help you with your luggage then," one called out. My mother responded that her son could handle the suitcase. "Where's the rest of it, Lydee?" asked the Australian. When my mother responded there was no "rest of it," they began to take her seriously. Here was a woman about to take a long, hard train ride with two children, and all she was bringing was a single canvas bag.

My mother, ever prepared, had used a Scopolamine patch, and had given me half a pill for seasickness before we left the dock. My sister, who by the age of seven had been exposed to a multitude of foreign bacteria and numerous stomach-churning modes of transportation, had a cast iron stomach and never suffered motion sickness. Everyone else, including many of the crew, became deathly ill. The boat ride was horrible. For three days and two nights we bounced around like a cork in the swirling waters of one of the most tumultuous seas on our planet.

Due to both heavy swells and cross currents, there were few people in the dining room our first evening on board. A waitress bringing a tureen of borsch to the table watched in horror as a wave came up to the port side portholes and caused half the contents of the tureen to hit the starboard wall. The next wave crashed over the top of the boat causing chaos as the boat bobbed back up out of the water. When the remaining soup hit the ceiling and a large Australian landed on my mother's lap, we left the dining room. Mom, Zoe and I thumped down corridors careening off walls and avoiding stairs which either went up or down depending on the angle of the boat, and finally made it to the entertainment room.

That night we made makeshift beds in the entertainment room because everyone was sick below deck in the sleeping rooms. When a particularly strong wave smashed into the boat, the piano slid across the room and broke through a cabinet that contained dishes and musical instruments. We barely escaped being hit by the spray of glass and an airborne clarinet. My mother and I helped two green-looking Japanese stewards clean up the glass and rope the piano to the wall. They had a large roll of plastic with them with which they were trying to cover the hallways as the vomiting seemed to be getting out of hand. However, the next time the boat lurched they abandoned the project and fled. Zoe enjoyed riding the plastic roll like a horse as it slid from one end of the room to the other.

On the second day, my mother commanded the Japanese cook to give her containers of miso soup, and told me to take them to the Australians in the sleeping rooms below deck. I put the containers of soup in my backpack and attempted to go down the stairs. The boat pitched violently, and suddenly stairs that had been going down turned into horizontal stairs across the starboard wall. I gripped the handrails and hung in mid-air until the stairs pointed down again so I could descend. The dehydrated Australians were grateful for the soup.

The boat finally docked in Vladivostok. When the Australians staggered onto the dock, my mother, barely suppressing a grin, told Zoe and me to help them with their luggage.

The Big Train Ride
The Trans-Siberian Railroad is one of the world's great train rides. We boarded the train in Vladivostok, and rode through ten time-zones before we arrived in Moscow. The ever-vigilant Soviet Union was allowing small groups of travelers on the train only if accompanied by a "tour guide." Olga, our guide (and KGB agent), knew more about asking pertinent questions than she did about the terrain we were crossing. "Why," she would ask my mother, "Why would a woman who lives in Canada and holds an American passport travel across Siberia with two children and no husband?" My mother responded that the only way to make peace with an adversary was to know them, understand their culture and appreciate their art, music and literature. My mother explained that she chose to come to the Soviet Union during the Cold War so that her children could learn about one of the world's great countries from its own people. Olga was not satisfied with the answer, and the questions kept coming.

Olga was everywhere. She told us not to take photographs of trains, train stations, airplanes, buildings, schools, factories, tanks, boats, policemen or the military. She warned us that even though the schedule that was taped to the bathroom door of our carriage said the train would stop for twenty minutes in each town, in actuality the train would leave when its business was completed, thereby rendering the schedule completely useless. She told us that we could leave the train and buy food from the vendors at any stop, but we were not to stray too far, as the train would leave without warning. No conductor would call. No whistle would sound. It would just leave.

After a few hours in our crowded compartment, we were eager to stretch our legs, and we joined the Australians who jumped on the platform before the train came to a complete halt. We bought cucumbers, berries, and cold, soggy fried potatoes from old women who wore colorful scarves on their heads and sold food out of ancient, but sturdy looking, baby carriages they rolled up and down the platform. We were ever vigilant, and as the train began to move we called to each other and jumped on. I would help my mom on, hand Zoe to her, and then grab a railing and swing myself aboard, James Bond style.

One afternoon Zoe had fallen asleep and my mother asked me to get off at the next station and look for any kind of fruit. I spent too much time looking and didn't notice the train beginning to move. My mother almost had a heart attack when she looked out of the window and saw me running alongside the train as fast as I could to grab the railing. Mom asked Olga what would happen if anyone missed the train. "Nothing good," was Olga's reply.

The carriage we were on had a long aisle down one side and several sleeping compartments on the other. At one end of the carriage was a samovar with hot water in it, and at the other end was the bathroom. The bathroom consisted of a small sink with a cold water tap, no soap, no towels and no toilet. Instead of a toilet, it had a small hole in the floor that you had to squat over, and your waste fell directly onto the tracks. There was a sign in Russian that must have said not to use the bathrooms in the train stations because nobody did.

Two benches faced each other in our very small compartment. Above them were platforms that were held to the wall by leather straps and could be lowered to sleep on at night. The two benches and platforms had two-inch mattress pads. I slept on the top platform, mom and Zoe slept below me, and two Australian men slept across from us. My mother rejected the dirty blankets they gave us, and we slept in our jackets. Zoe used our dirty clothes bag as a pillow.

There was a window and a small table between the benches. It was tight. Every night Olga put her head into the compartment to count us and to remind us "Nyet photos in the night!" One night I wished her a "Good Nyet" and the Australians, mom and Zoe howled with laughter. Olga didn't understand our humor and just shook her head. After that all of us wished her "Good Nyet" every night and it made us laugh every time.

The first day we were on the train, my mom and I tried to open the window as it was getting uncomfortably hot in our compartment. We tugged at it for a while, and then the two Australians came to our aid. The four of us were finally able to wrench the window open a full eight inches just as we rode into a tunnel. Clouds of smoke from the coal burning engine poured into our compartment, and it took us twice as long to raise the window because the four of us were gasping for breath and laughing so hard. Olga, ever-patrolling our carriage, heard us and ran into our room. We were black, the walls were black, the bedding was black and the five of us were howling with laughter. "Silly people, silly people, always check the engine. If it is electric, then you open your window," she barked, "if it is coal you do not!" To her amazement, we laughed even harder.

We discovered that in the night some carriages would leave our train and others would be added. It was not uncommon to go to sleep three cars from the dining room, and then have to travel 20 cars to find it in the morning. To further confuse the passengers, we wouldn't know in which direction to begin looking for the dining car. Moving from car to car involved opening a very heavy door, jumping from the moving metal plate of one car to that of the next, and then throwing your weight against the door to the next car. My mother always took at least two Australians with her when we went on expeditions to find the ever-moving dining car. The first Australian would jump to the platform of the next car and the second would toss Zoe across the moving plates to him. They gently helped my mother across the access way, but I enjoyed the leap.

I awoke one morning with a headache because the Russians in the compartments at the far end of our carriage had been drinking and singing all night, and the entire carriage smelled of vodka, cigarette smoke and sweaty soldiers. It was a cold Siberian morning and the terrain was monotonous. Due to the permafrost, all the trees were dwarfed and the buildings, fences and posts were at odd angles. Zoe was making a lot of noise playing ball with a hung-over Russian sergeant in the hallway, and I was beginning to feel a little sick to my stomach. I stood in a long line to get into the bathroom where I splashed cold water on my face, but the smell in there made me run back to our compartment.

Once in our compartment, I tried to open the window, but it was stuck closed — stuck open was its other position. Just then Olga knocked on the door and announced that all cameras should be put away immediately. My mother and I joined the Australians in the hall, and we all caught a glimpse of Russian fighter planes flying in formation over acres of tanks. We were traveling through a restricted zone.

Olga marched us off to lunch and, unfortunately, sat at our table. It is so boring eating with a KGB agent who never stops asking questions. I knew she had her eye on me because the day before she had caught me taking a picture of a drunk Russian man, and she would have busted me had I not given her the Ray Bradbury book I had just finished reading. Lunch did nothing to quell my upset stomach because I found three dandelion buds, a bay leaf and a rock in my borsch. I felt miserable and wished I had stayed in our compartment and photographed the fighter planes.

We enjoyed photographing the many Siberian cities we visited, and we became more accustomed to the long, long train rides between them. Olga was always there to keep a vigilant eye on us and to remind us which photographs not to take. I felt invincible, as I had already photographed Soviet tanks and fighter planes from the window of our compartment. However, after I saw a policeman in plain clothes take the camera away from one of the Australians, open it, expose the film and hand it back to him, I became more cautious. I hid behind pillars, posts and statues. I stood behind my mother and squeezed the telephoto lens between her neck and her long hair. I photographed trains, train stations, airplanes, buildings, schools, factories, tanks, boats, policemen and a surfacing submarine, but I didn't photograph the soldiers because my mother beat me to it.

While wandering around the city of Irkutsk with six Australians, we came across some very powerful proletarian statues. A group of soldiers in uniform were gathered on some nearby steps and their captain was taking their picture. My mother walked up to the Australians, who had become ever so cautious about taking pictures, and bet them 30 rubles each that she could photograph the soldiers. Their money came out of their pockets really fast. My mom walked up to the captain and, gesticulating furiously, said, "I want to photo your army!"

The man replied, "Nyet photo army," turned his back to her, and began to readjust his lens. I have never known my mother to take "nyet" for an answer.

"Nyet," she said, "I want to photo your army and my baby." At which point she dragged Zoe into the middle of the front row of soldiers.

"Nyet," the man repeated and began to take a picture of Zoe with his men.

"Nyet, and hold it," said mom, "You photo my baby, I photo your army."

"Da," he responded, and their shutters clattered simultaneously.

Mom smiled at me, and I gathered the money.

Lake Baikal

The train took us to Irkutsk, a cold — even in summer — town, near the banks of Lake Baikal. Geologists date the lake to be 30 million years old, making it the oldest lake in the world. Most people know this lake as the deepest lake in the world.

A drafty old bus took us to the shore of Lake Baikal and deposited us by a rusting hydrofoil. When my mother spotted the hydrofoil, she immediately tried to talk the Australians into going out on the lake with us. Because she couldn't swim, she figured the Australians could dive into the freezing water and save us should we capsize, but of course she didn't tell them that. The Australians were reluctant to go. "It's bloody big," said one of them when he heard the lake was 395 miles long and 80 miles wide. "It's bloody deep," said another when he heard the lake was over a mile in depth. It looked like a no go.

But my mom, determined to experience this 23,000 cubic kilometers of water from other than the shore, herded Zoe and me onto the hydrofoil and yelled down to the Australians, "Get your bloody selves into this bloody hydrofoil before I tell the bloody world that you let a single mother, a little boy and a young girl child go on it alone." With a great amount of reluctance they boarded the boat.

After a couple of false starts, some jerking and a grinding sound we were skimming above a lake that held 20% of the world's unfrozen fresh water. In the winter the ice freezes 28-45 inches thick, and during the winters when track was being laid for the Trans-Siberian Railroad, the train was run over the lake.

Moscow

Moscow is an amazing city. It was founded in 1147 and it is now home to ten million people. Everything is big. There are 30 million books in the library, and there are many huge proletarian sculptures commemorating the Great Patriotic War in which 23 million people died. We marched up and down Red Square, viewed the intricately beautiful St. Basil's Church, and were able to go into the unrestricted areas of the Kremlin. When Zoe mistakenly called it the Gremlin even Olga laughed. I enjoyed the Space Monument and the Space Pavilion, even though they confiscated my camera at the door. The GUM Department store was huge and over a million people a day came to buy what looked like twenty-year-old merchandise. The Metro was impressive. Sliding walkways took us down to the subway level where the walls were lined with fine art, and beautiful crystal chandeliers hung from the ceiling. My mother agreed with me that this was a perfect place for a museum for it had such a wide audience.

Zoe and I were awakened at 5:00 a.m. by our mother, who told us to dress quickly and not say a word. The three of us sneaked out of our hotel and, at last free of Olga, took off on our own to photograph Moscow. These were perhaps the best photographs of our trip. I took a picture of mom and Zoe reflected in a puddle. We saw a large statue of Lenin and sat Zoe on his lap. While I looked around for police, mom quickly took the picture. We spent a wonderful morning laughing and photographing with complete freedom.

Leningrad (now St. Petersburg)

We took a nine-hour train ride from Moscow to Leningrad so that my mother could at last view the Rembrandt in the Hermitage. The Hermitage was built in 1754 by Empress Catherine II because she wanted Russia to compete artistically with the European nations. She commissioned 4,000 workers to build a winter palace that would contain 460 rooms and take eight years to complete. The patronage of Catherine the Great enabled artists, architects and sculptors to flourish and, because of her, mid-18th-century Russia experienced a renaissance in art.

Catherine II also commissioned and collected art from Europe. She filled her winter palace with prints, drawings, sculpture, engraved gems and cameos, ivory, coins, porcelain, precious metals, mosaics, stained glass, arms and armor, ceramics, jewelry, painted miniatures, furniture and carriages. She kept enlarging the building and adding to her collection even after her palace became the largest museum in the world. Catherine called her winter palace The Hermitage because it was a place where she could retire and view her massive collection in privacy. After the revolution, The Hermitage was opened to the public so the Russian people could enjoy one of the world's greatest art collections.

The Hermitage was huge and contained three million objects of art. We saw Rembrandts, sculptures by Da Vinci and paintings by

Raphael and assorted other great masters. One extremely gilded room with intricately inlaid floors held a very large table and a mammoth vase made entirely of lapis lazuli. After a few hours of dragging my sister and me through room after room after room of art treasures, even my mother became overwhelmed and we headed back to our hotel.

That night we went to the theatre. We saw a varied program that featured fantastic Russian dances, beautiful ballet and a clown act. What I found most interesting was that the Russians applauded in unison and at an increasing tempo which resulted in a thunderous and powerful applause. We adapted our undisciplined applause to match theirs. When we were finished clapping, the performers clapped in unison to acknowledge the audience.

Checkpoint Charlie

All the trains in Europe run on standard-gauge tracks that are 4' 8 1/2" apart. The trains in the Soviet Union run on broad-gauge tracks that are 4' 11 7/8" apart. The difference in the gauge of the tracks has prevented the Soviet Union from being invaded by train during wars.

When our train left the Soviet Union and entered East Germany, it rolled into an enclosed station where each car was lifted into the air by a stationary crane. The bogies, the mechanism on the bottom of each car that contains the wheels, brakes and the apparatus that allows them to turn, had to be replaced to accommodate the narrower European track.

Olga knocked on the door of our carriage, and before we could open it she shrieked, "All cameras put away! All cameras put away!" Mom, Zoe and I bounded into the hall and looked out of the window to watch another car lifted into the air while the bogies were changed and then lowered onto the new track. As we watched, Olga marched behind us chanting, "No cameras. No cameras here. No cameras."

The train stopped at several checkpoints before we reached West Germany. Men with stern looks and polished boots boarded the train and examined each passenger's travel documents. Evidently we were suspect because we lived in Canada and traveled with U.S. passports and there was no man with us. But what really made them suspect us was that the three of us were traveling with only one canvas bag. At one checkpoint, two men entered our carriage, pointed to our single suitcase and shouted at my mother in German. When she didn't respond they looked under our bed, ripped the bedding off our mattress, turned the mattress over, and dumped the contents of our suitcase, my backpack and my mom's purse on it. And then they left. I couldn't tell if my mother was angry, nervous or a combination of both, but I could see her hands were shaking as she repacked our bag.

It was past midnight when the train pulled into Check Point Charlie, the last and most difficult checkpoint we would go through. Before the men boarded the train, my mom handed me the travel documents, told me to deal with the officials politely, got on the bed with my sleeping sister and pretended she was asleep. When the men entered our carriage, I handed them the documents. They looked at my sleeping mother and sister hugging each other, hesitated a moment, examined the documents and left. A few minutes later we rolled into West Germany.

AUSTRALIA

Zoe is nine and I am seventeen

They actually say "G'day" in Australia. They crinkle a lot of other words and say "Barbie" instead of barbecue, "Crissy presses" instead of Christmas presents and "lollys" instead of candy. The first problem we encountered when we landed in Sidney was that Australia is so large we didn't know where to go or how to get there. Our best course of action was to go to a travel agent and ask what our "oppies" were. "Oppies" is what they say instead of options.

Always on a tight budget, my mother outdid herself this time and found a bankrupt tour company that had to take one last tour to fulfill its obligation to its staff, most of whom were the children of the owners. Most tourists backed away when they heard this was the company's last trip. My mother, however, was the first to sign up. We were stranded in Sydney for a week while the tour company beat the bushes for a few more guests to justify putting their big bus on the road. That was good for us because Sydney was a wonderful city in which to be stranded.

The best way to discover what the city of Sydney has to offer is to buy a ticket for the Sydney Explorer Bus that stops at 26 points of interest. Between each stop the driver gives tourists a running commentary on the next attraction. Buying a ticket allows you to hop on and off the bus whenever you want and stay there as long as you want as another Explorer Bus will cruise by every fifteen minutes. In this way we were able to get the lay of the land and stake out the places we wanted to explore for the rest of the week.

Our first choice was the Sydney Opera house, designed by the Danish architect Jorn Utzon and completed in 1973. This fine building is set on pilings that jut out into Sydney's beautiful harbor. By the time Utzon finished the shell of the opera house he had spent 100 million dollars, and was so over budget that they didn't allow him to design the interior. We spent a few minutes inside the opera house. My mother found it pretty but uninspired compared to the outside. By now I was becoming an accomplished photographer and the lines and planes of this building set against a piercing blue sky were exciting to photograph. While I was taking pictures, mom and Zoe enjoyed a picnic lunch and watched the boat traffic in the busy harbor. Zoe busied herself by saying "G'day mate" to tourists who were more than happy to respond to the smiling Australian child. She even posed with them, and smiled widely when they took her picture.

Sydney is Australia's most progressive and energetic city. We enjoyed eating in little cafes in the predominantly gay part of town at night. During the day we spent most of our time in museums. In one museum we saw the magnificent Elgin Marbles that had been taken from the Parthenon in Greece 200 years ago. In another, we saw rooms filled with skeletons. There was a human skeleton, several dinosaur skeletons and skeletons of everyday common animals. Zoe was fascinated by a snake skeleton and I by a cat's skeleton. Mom hung out with the bear's skeleton for a while, but had to agree that the cat's skeleton looked as if it belonged to a miniature dinosaur and was so remarkable that she would never look at a cat again without thinking about its skeleton.

By the end of the week the tour bus was outfitted and we were ready to go. There were only eighteen guests, two drivers, a cook and a travel guide. We brought our own sleeping bags, and the company supplied the tents and the food. There were so few of us that each guest took up a row of seats and Zoe and I had the entire back of the bus to ourselves. Our seven-week camping trip would take us up the east coast through Victoria, New South Wales and Queensland, to the Northern Territories, and down the middle through South Australia. We would sleep in the outback every night and visit the towns of Brisbane, Caring, Darwin, Alice Springs, Adelaide and

Melbourne. When the bus took off, all eighteen passengers cheered and the crew, happy that they had one last trip, led us in Australia's true national anthem "Waltzing Matilda." Mom, Zoe and I smiled as we realized this would be a very easy summer.

At night we slept under the foreign stars of the southern hemisphere. The Southern Cross replaced our big and little dippers, but the most astonishing thing was that the half and quarter moons, instead of being vertical, were horizontal, making them look like celestial smiles. Wedge-tailed eagles flew above us and wild dingoes scampered behind our tents. Our outback appetites made up for the mediocre food, and we went to bed each night anticipating the adventures the next day would hold.

The east coast of Australia is comprised of endless beaches, remarkable rock formations and subtropical rain forests. We saw fish, dolphins and whales leaping out of the blue-green water, and the sea-washed air filled our lungs with the salt smell of the ocean. Many Australian miles later we came to Queensland and the Great Barrier Reef, Australia's most famous natural wonder.

There are over 1,000 islands in this delicate ecosystem that has evolved over hundreds of thousands of years and contains over 6,000 species of plants and fish. We boarded a helicopter, and as we flew over the Great Barrier Reef we could see the top of it, just inches below the ocean's surface, its body extending iceberg-like down into the sea. The helicopter landed on a raft, and we were able to walk around and examine the reef more closely.

While Zoe and mom peered at the living coral and thousands of multicolored, tropical fish through a glass-bottom boat, I dove off the side, swam beneath it and plastered myself against the glass causing my mom, Zoe and the other tourists to scream. When my mother regained her composure, she made me do it again and took a picture of me spread-eagled under the glass. The days we spent exploring the mysterious east coast were so wonderful that it was difficult to get back on the bus and to the never-ending road again.

The red dust road sliced through endless aboriginal lands, and we drove for miles and miles and miles through the desolate outback. Whenever we saw a gas station we filled our tank because sometimes stations were 300 miles apart. There was no speed limit, and huge trucks called road-trains, hauling several attached trailers, roared past us at incredible speeds. The road-trains had large iron grates called roo-catchers mounted on their front bumpers so that the many kangaroos they hit would not damage their radiators. Thousands of miles of desolate road cut through the sparsely-populated center of the continent, and after a few days we settled into a rhythm with the endless road, the turning wheels, the big sky and the hot dusty air.

At noon we pulled off the road for lunch that consisted of white bread, sandwich meats, potato salad, hard boiled eggs and pickles spread out on two unsteady card tables. The instant we got off the bus we were swarmed by flies. Zoe and I ran around the bus while eating our sandwiches in an effort to keep flies away from our faces. Mom covered herself with tiger balm and smelled so strong that she kept not only the flies but the rest of us away from her.

Flies, however, weren't the only creatures we attracted. One afternoon a group of four emus came toward us as we were finishing our lunch. The cook quickly gathered the leftover food and dashed into the bus with it. Emus are flightless birds that look like very large ostriches gone strange. They are covered with thick, drooping feathers that look more like fur, have long necks and long legs, grow to be about six feet tall, and don't look very bright.

I still had a sandwich in my hand and one of the emus had its eye on it. The bus driver told us that an emu will go away if it thinks you are taller than it is. He added that they are so stupid that if you raise your hand above your head they will think you are really tall and run away. So when a mid-sized emu came toward me, I raised the hand in which I was holding my sandwich above my head. The emu looked at me quizzically, determined that my extended hand was higher than its head and backed away a couple of steps. It then coiled its long neck and quickly extended it, hitting me in my armpit. I bent over in shock and pain lowering the sandwich and allowing the emu to snatch it. As the emu ran off with it, everyone laughed, Zoe took a picture, and mom said I probably met one of the smartest emus in Australia.

In the evening, while we set up our tents among the gum trees, curious kangaroos hopped within a few feet of us to see what we were doing. Zoe begged the cook for bread and quietly sat in the bush until baby kangaroos, called joeys, hopped up to her and nibbled the bread from her hand. Mom explained that kangaroos, as well as wallabies and koalas, are marsupials, animals that carry their young in pouches. The cook told us that males are called boomers and females, flyers. She added, kangaroos travel in groups called mobs that can vary from a few dozen to several hundred. They drink very little water and can live without it for months. The bus driver told us that when the European explorers came to Australia they were shocked by these strange animals that can weigh up to 175 pounds, hop up to 40 mph and jump as high as ten feet. He said that the longest kangaroo leap recorded was 20 feet. When the explorers asked the aborigines what the animals were called, the aborigines answered, "kangaroo" which meant, "I don't understand that question."

Darwin

In the Northern Territories, at the very northern tip of Australia, lies the town of Darwin. This is a town of true survivors, because Darwin is a tough place to live. Small signs on the beaches on the outskirts of town warn tourists not to swim because of small fish that appear in the summer. If bitten, a swimmer could die within fifteen minutes. Their bites were deadly because the nearest hospital is hours away. Cyclones batter the northern coast with treacherous regularity. In 1974, Cyclone Tracy all but destroyed the town. An "I" beam, twisted by the cyclone like a corkscrew stands in the center of town — a monument to the amazing destructive power of wind and rain and to the brave people who still live there.

A few months before we came to Darwin, a man who had been released from the hospital found a crocodile next to his car in the hospital parking lot. He was so frightened that he had a heart attack and had to be readmitted. Many of the residents of Darwin have equally horrific crocodile stories.

The aboriginal people in the Northern Territories date back 40,000 years and are considered one of the world's oldest people. My mother told us that only a few generations ago some of the indigenous people in the Australian outback lived in stone-age conditions without fire. It is little wonder that in Australia there exists a tremendous cultural clash between the settlers and the aboriginal people. Even today, some young aboriginal men "go walkabout." They leave their jobs and families and go on a solitary journey through the outback for an indeterminate amount of time to discover their own strengths. This journey holds great spiritual significance for them and is easily misunderstood by many non-aboriginals.

Alice Springs

Our bus began to tilt to the right a few hundred miles outside of Alice Springs, a small town that sits in the very center of the continent. Everyone became suddenly silent and pensive, because the thought of breaking down in the outback was a bit frightening. "So much for an easy vacation," I said to my mother. By some miracle, we made it to Alice Springs just before the suspension expired completely.

Alice Springs is a charming outback town that has been called the heart of Australia. The day we arrived they were advertising camel and lizard races. Unfortunately, we missed both as we had to pitch our camp on the outskirts of town for a few days while the suspension was being repaired. The crew and I rented motorbikes and explored the town and surrounding areas. It was fun driving on the opposite side of the road, but making a right hand turn was a bit dangerous at first. My mom spent two days finding a man who would take the three of us into the outback on camels.

Zoe, who was an ardent animal lover, came to life the minute she saw her surly looking camel, and laughed with joy as it slowly rose to a standing position with her on its back. "Don't they have some sort of seat belts," my mother called to the man as the camel Zoe was on walked away from the rest of us at a brisk pace in an easterly direction. The flea-ridden camel I was to ride spit at me the minute I walked toward it. I was hesitant to get on the beast, but thought I should, as Zoe seemed to be leaving us. When the camel finally stood up, I jerked it around until it pointed at the rear of Zoe's camel. Nothing happened, so I kind of kicked it. My camel jolted and ran, and suddenly I was riding next to Zoe, both of us in an easterly direction. The camel man yelled and screamed at us to return, but the steering part of the ride was over. The beasts had minds of their own. He finally had to ride over and haul us back.

In the meantime, my mother was realizing why camels are called the ships of the desert. Horses lead with their right front leg and their left rear leg, followed by their left front leg and their right rear leg. This gives the rider a relatively smooth ride. Camels, on the other hand, kind of float through the sand leading with their right front and back leg, followed by their left front and back leg. This makes the rider sway as if riding on waves. Within a few miles, my mother was experiencing seasickness in the middle of the desert.

Long-limbed gum trees shimmered silver in the heat against the sapphire sky as the camels took us through huge eroded sand dunes and sandstone outcroppings. Our guide skirted us past termite mounds that stood four feet tall and resembled the top half of huge beehives. Out of nowhere, we came upon some craggy rocks and cliffs that held pockets of vegetation. The aboriginal people we met smiled at us and waved, seemingly happy to see tourists away from the beaten path experiencing the true down under. The camel man told us that they were the Lurijta people whose culture dated back 20,000 years.

That night the camel man took us to a Corroboree, a gathering of aboriginal people who perform traditional sacred dances. We saw the dancers make ancient designs on their bodies with red ocher and crushed white flower blossoms. Then they danced the Dream Time Dance and circled each other stamping their feet in the red sand to the beat of the boomerang clap sticks and the haunting sound of the didgeridoo. The dancers chanted ancient stories and sang to the possum in their native language. The possum, my mother explained, is God's messenger on earth. The aboriginal people tell their wishes to the possum who climbs a tree and tells the raven, who flies to heaven and tells God. The dance was hypnotic and soon the few people in the audience were swaying with the music. Zoe was asleep, her head in mom's lap, with a smile on her face.

The next day, the bus was ready and we were on the road again. Our first stop was a tourist attraction where a man wrestled crocodiles and admonished the kids in the audience, "Don't do this at home!" My mom was so upset by the crocodile in captivity that we barely heard a word the man was saying. She stopped talking, however, when he told the audience that crocodiles pounce on their victims, lock their jaws, plunge them underwater and do a death roll that both disorients and batters their prey. He said that many times crocodiles will jam their catch under a log, wait for it to rot and soften, and consume it days later. He told us that freshwater crocodiles could live in only fresh water, but saltwater crocodiles could live in both fresh and salt water. They have been seen 2,000 miles inland. I could tell by my mother's rapt attention that she would be checking out our campsites for crocodiles for the remainder of the trip.

The next part of the show dealt with poisonous snakes: how to spot them, how to harvest their venom and how to survive their bites. The look on my mother's face told me that she would be looking for snakes as well as crocodiles. He finished his show by throwing a rubber snake into the audience and making everyone scream. On the way back to the bus a nervous lady saw a dusty stick in the road. I pointed to it and jokingly said, "Look a snake." She screamed and jumped onto my back causing both of us to fall on top of the innocent stick. My mother and Zoe didn't stop laughing for about fifty miles.

We drove by burning sugar cane fields that sent plumes of black smoke across the wide horizon and filled the air with an acrid smell. Scorched red deserts gave way to canyons and gorges where water seemed to spring from nowhere and flowed hurriedly to somewhere else. We took a boat ride down the Ormistra Gorge to view the ancient rock paintings, called petroglyphs, on its walls. My mother, ever scanning the water for crocodiles, missed most of the rock art, but Zoe and I filled her in later.

It is so hot in the Australian outback that most of the buildings are built with a large airspace beneath them. In the outback, it is illegal to have a pub that is not attached to a hotel. Every once in a while, we would drive by a lone building in the middle of nowhere that was a pub/hotel. One night we camped within earshot of an outback pub and could hear an amazing amount of noise coming from the place. Mom and the cook went pubbing that night, while underage Zoe and I had to stay in our tent. When she came back a couple of hours later she had lots to tell us.

She told us that the pub had two entrances, one for the non-aboriginals and the other for everyone else, but after a little while people were so drunk that they all seemed to stagger out of the door nearest them. There was a man stationed on the porch who pointed people toward the steps so they wouldn't fall off the edge of the porch. The pub's customers were locals from miles around, as well as a good number of road-train drivers. The few women in the pub drank as hard as the men and held their own in raucous stories and songs. Mom said she saw a furry clump of something on the floor and later discovered it was the hair from a very drunk bald man's head. Evidently he had lost some sort of drinking game and had forfeited his hair. The bartender told my mom that the bald man, who had a few clumps of hair sticking out and a great number of bloody scratches on his head was going to be married the next day. Mom told us that if they filmed a movie in that place nobody would believe it.

Uluru

Many red dirt miles later we came to Uluru. Uluru, called Ayers Rock by non-aboriginals, is a monolith that extends 1150 feet above the ground and is nearly six miles in circumference. It is the largest rock in the world, and stands alone in the flat, red desert that surrounds it. Uluru is a sacred site for the aboriginal people and its sides and caves are decorated with ancient petroglyphs. What makes this rock even more remarkable is that more than two thirds of it lies underground—an iceberg turned to stone.

Our first morning there Zoe, mom and I joined five other people to climb to the top of the great rock. A plaque at the base of Uluru commemorates those who have died climbing it and cautions climbers not to reach for their hats if they blow off, or chase their lens caps if they roll away from them. A series of posts connects a chain to the top, and climbers are instructed not to let go of the chain for any reason. Three quarters of the way to the top, such a strong wind came up that Zoe found it hard to hang on to the chain. She and mom hid in a convenient cave to wait out the wind while I continued to the top.

The 360-degree view from the top was spectacular. We could see the flat ground extend for miles in every direction. Uluru stood absolutely alone. It was little wonder to me that this lone stone in the middle of nowhere held deep spiritual significance for the aboriginal people. On the way down, another climber and I helped Zoe and mom with the difficult descent.

That night we watched Uluru change color as the sun set. The huge monolith changed from a bright orange/red daytime color to a deeper amber, then to a red/brown that faded to a blue/brown, then to purple and suddenly to black as the sun set. The next morning, mom had a surprise for me. She had booked a seat on a small Cessna that would fly me over Uluru and the surrounding areas. I was thrilled, and later in my life, when I became a pilot, I would remember every detail of that very special flight.

Uluru might have been the biggest rock in the world, but there were other amazing rock formations in the outback. In the middle of miles of scorched, red earth we came upon the Olgas — 36 dome-shaped peaks just sitting there. The aborigines called the Olgas "The Place of Many Heads," and in the night they did look like the heads of a group of balding men bent toward each other talking.

The Devil's Marbles were a collection of enormous round granite boulders, one split exactly in half, some balanced on top of each other, others just a roll away. A geologist could probably have told us what they were made of and how they got there, but my mom much preferred to take the name literally and assume that the Devil had just left them behind.

One Hundred Miles From Coober Pedy

The bus stopped and we set up our tents a hundred miles from the town of Coober Pedy, at what seemed to me to be the most desolate spot on earth. It was flat, it was hot, it was horrible. An abandoned gas pump, a testimonial to someone's failure to make a go of it in this Godforsaken place, stood alone against the sunset. The bus driver told us that several Hollywood movies depicting the end of the world after World War III had been filmed in the area. The earth was red, the dust was red, the floor of our tent and the sandwiches we ate were red. Zoe and I agreed this was the worst place we had ever been.

My mother, however, was transported to a state of bliss by this miserable place. She spent a roll of film photographing the lone gas pump from every conceivable angle—both Zoe and I declined invitations to stand next to it. Then she set out to explore the area by herself. "I'm going walkabout," she said.

"Not even the kangaroos like this place. What's wrong with mom?" Zoe asked me. It didn't take us long to find out because when mom returned, covered by a thick film of red dust, she told us.

"This is the most remarkable place I have ever been," she said. "There is absolutely nothing here — no hills, no trees, no plants, no views. There is nothing here. If you take water away from a place you have a desert — even the bottom of the sea without water is a desert. Then, if you take away the topography and the plants, this is what you get. There is nothing here to camouflage you, and nothing to hide behind. This is a place of intense honesty. There is absolutely nothing here!"

Zoe and I ate dinner with the rest of the people, while mom sat next to the gas pump and watched the sun set. After dinner, Zoe and I rolled our sleeping bags out in the tent and fell asleep. Mom didn't join us for a very long time. The next day when the rest of us were leaping on the bus with joy. I could tell my mother was reluctant to leave. As she stood by the gas pump for the last time, the bus driver told me that many of the aboriginal people who travel past here have the same reaction my mother was having. He said that the aboriginal people think of this ancient land as some kind of a mystic power spot.

The bus driver told us that Willy Hutchinson was fifteen years old in 1915 when he discovered an opal while walking through the Australian outback. It didn't take long for prospectors to arrive, stake claims and tear up the land looking for the semi-precious stones. He told us that opals are found within a few dozen feet of the surface making strip mining the easiest way to get them. Odd looking machines called diggers unearth the dirt, and blowers throw it up into the air thereby sifting the sand away from the harder rocks that hold the opals.

That place was known as the Stewart Range Opal Field and was located in the driest part of the driest state on the driest continent on earth. And it was hot. It was so hot that the miners and their families lived in underground homes to escape the heat. By 1922, a small town had sprung up to service the miners, and its residents decided the place needed a proper name. The aborigines called the town "Kupa Piti" and so the residents decided to adapt that name, and called their town Coober Pedy. Only years later did they realize that "Kupa Piti" meant "white men in holes." The main street of this town is named after Willy Hutchinson.

Today Coober Pedy mines 75% of the world's opals, and half of the people who live in this harsh outback town live underground. We visited their underground church for about three minutes until my mom discovered she was claustrophobic and fled. The land is flat and devoid of vegetation, and mining has left constantly shifting piles of dirt as far as the eye can see. Zoe kept asking if we were on the moon. She wasn't far off because a few years later this eerie landscape would be used in many science fiction films.

Australia was big. Everything about it was big: the Great Barrier Reef, the sapphire sky, the deep red gorges, the huge monolith-rocks, the vast horizon, the scorched red earth and the endless highway. We covered so many miles and we had so many adventures, but the Australian outback was what captured our hearts and our imaginations. They call the outback the land of never never because they say once you truly explore it you will never, never want to leave.

AFRICA

Zoe is nine and I am seventeen

We were taught to conserve water and not waste food. We joined our mother in campaigns to save forests and endangered species. We were a thrifty and eco-sensitive family. However, in an effort to develop our artistic abilities, our mother told us that we should consider paper, colored pens, paints, scotch tape and film to be free. We were told that their supply was inexhaustible, and we were encouraged to use them even frivolously. She put cameras in our hands as soon as we were able to hold them, and took delight in the out-of-focus, oddly tilted photographs we took. Zoe and I fought for the camera when we traveled, and the clattering sound of the shutter accompanied us everywhere. Nowhere did we take more pictures than in Africa.

On Safari

The best way to experience Africa is to go on safari. The cost of a safari varies greatly. The most expensive ones house guests in luxurious, walled resorts. During the day they travel in air-conitioned buses. Sumptuous lunches are set for them on mesas where they can view the grazing herds. Tables are set with white linen tablecloths, silver flatware and crystal stemware, and stately Africans in white jackets wait upon them. Back at the resort they are treated to a dinner buffet that rivals fine European dining.

Ours was the least expensive safari consisting of a fifteen-seat bus with a pop-top roof and bald tires. Following it was another bus that contained ripped tents, kettles on tripods that hung over campfires, and as many cooks as could fit into the bus. Because economic conditions are so poor and jobs so sparse, many people are hired, and paid poorly, to do any given job. Our safari, even though it was the least expensive, was comprised of ten guests and fifteen servants.

My mother contended that life began in Africa, and this was our pilgrimage back to our true roots. Like Islamic people who make a pilgrimage to Mecca, she seemed to be in a state of religious bliss the moment we arrived in Kenya. She barely listened to me when I pointed out the bald tires on the bus, and she hardly noticed that evening when I patched our badly torn tent with the roll of duct tape we carried in our canvas bag.

It was early evening when we arrived at our first campsite. The multitude of cooks began setting a fire for our evening meal as a tall Masai warrior made sure we set up our tents fiteeen paces apart in a circle, and another set smaller fires that would burn throughout the night to keep the animals away. I asked Nicholas, our driver, why the tents were so far apart. That night when I told my mother we were fifteen paces from the neighboring tents so the elephants could pass through the camp without crushing us, she frantically put Zoe's sleeping bag between ours. When I teased Zoe that she was the cheese in an elephant sandwich, mom glared at me.

Africa never sleeps. When the sun goes down, the hyenas begin their long, silver screams and the night predators come out. Behind our tent, animals scurried, screamed, struggled and were eaten by animals that would eventually be eaten themselves. I was too worried to go to sleep just in case the tall silent Masai warriors who held spears and stood by the small fires fell asleep. I sat up and pinched my cheeks in order to keep awake all night so I could protect my sleeping mother and sister.

My mother woke me the next morning and dragged me out of the tent. There, outside our tent, was a two-foot-tall pile of elephant dung! We had been fast asleep when the elephants had walked through our campsite in the night.

We drove through a herd of 10,000 wildebeests, and lions slept in the shade of our bus. We pursued cheetahs and found their lairs, we hunted rhinoceroses and discovered their sleeping bogs, we stalked water buffalo and watched as they tended their young, we gave chase to giraffes and witnessed a newborn of only an hour or so escape a stalking lion. Nicholas taught us how to spot a nearly imperceptible movement in the high grass that marked the slow pace of a hunting female lion, and a small indentation where a male lion slept. Every day we hunted our prey, and every day we found them. We caught them in our sights and captured them on film.

One day we came upon a large herd of grazing gazelles, impalas and zebras. In their midst was a large male lion. Nicholas eased our fears for the vulnerable animals grazing mere feet from the lion. He explained that the lion had probably been asleep when the herd came upon him, and now it was he who was in danger. If he made a sudden move that frightened the herd, they would stampede and crush him beneath their hooves. We watched as the predator crept ever so slowly away from his prey.

One morning, my mom saw a cloud of vultures circling on the horizon. She asked Nicholas if he would take us to see them. The closer we got, the more intense the thunderous storm of black wings became. We stopped a few feet from the wildebeest upon which the vultures were feeding. Nicholas told us that in all probability the hyenas had brought down the animal, and fed as quickly as they could before the female lions came to claim the carrion. Now stripped of its flesh by the male and female lions, and then their cubs, the carcass was left for the vultures. Our mother, mesmerized by the carnage, sat silently as Zoe and I fought for the camera and photographed the scene. Vultures covered the carcass until it seemed alive with pulsating black wings. Featherless necks probed every cavity for bits of meat. In an attempt to consume a piece of flesh that clung to the inside of a rib, one greedy vulture folded back its wings and entered the wildebeest's rib cage. Ravenous vultures atop it pecked him to death and consumed his flesh as well. The sound of screeching vultures' flapping wings, and the breaking of small bones filled the air until the carcass was pecked clean. The moment the vultures took flight, the waiting hyenas returned to crack open the larger bones and suck their marrow. Splintered remains were left to swarms of insects to consume. The wildebeest was gone.

Wildebeests look as if they are made up of God's leftover parts. They have the shape of a large horse, the head of a donkey, and the hair of a buffalo. They make a high-pitched screeching sound that belies their bulk. Even the young are not darling. One evening, on the way back to our camp, we drove past a young wildebeest that was standing on an outcropping of rock. It had been somehow left behind the herd that was grazing in the valley below and was bleating for its mother. Zoe, upset that the young animal had been abandoned, asked Nicholas what was going to happen to him. Nicholas assured her that another herd was on its way and that he would be adopted by one of the female wildebeests. Twenty minutes later, when we arrived at our camp, my mother and I pulled Nicholas aside and asked about the young wildebeest. "Don't worry," replied Nicholas, "it's over."

The evening fires and vigilant Masai were constant reminders that we too were food. As we set out each morning on our ever-balding tires, I tried to imagine what would happen if we had a flat in the tall grasses where the lions slept. We had no phone, no radio, no gun, and we were surrounded by all those amazing animals that would eat us if we stepped out of the bus.

One morning as I rolled my sleeping bag, I noticed an odd-looking, dead bug beneath it that I must have rolled on and killed in the night. When I showed it to Nicholas, he said, "Scorpion, that's not good." I decided not to tell my mother about the scorpion until we were out of the bush, but after that I doubled my efforts to check out our tent and be sure mom and Zoe shook out their boots before they put them on every morning. Not only were we prey for the lions kept at bay by the Masai's fires, but also for insects that paid the fires no heed.

The Masai women shave their heads when they marry and consequently are fascinated by western women with hair. One morning, while mom was combing bits of twigs and leaves out of my sister's hair, a group of Masai women slowly approached them. I prepared myself for another "oh what a wonderful little foreign child" episode, but even I was captivated by my sister's long, auburn hair that caught the African sun and shimmered in its special morning light. My mother's welcoming smile gave courage to the women, and soon Zoe was once again surrounded by curious hands that touched and stroked her. I, on the other hand, was trying to figure out how I would make it through the rest of the safari, as my mother had given the Masai night guards one of my shirts and half of my socks.

Every day, and many, many times a day, Zoe and I photographed the most amazing array of animals. We saw three-foot impalas that survive by jumps up to ten feet in height and 30 feet in length; baboons that walk on all fours, bark like dogs and live in intricate social groups; buffalo that move in herds and behave so unpredictably that they are considered one of the most dangerous animals in Africa; cheetahs that can sprint up to 70 miles per hour and are the fastest animals in the world; elephants whose females live in family units and drive the young male juveniles away to join bachelor herds; giraffes that are born five feet tall, grow to eighteen feet and weigh up to a ton; hippopotamuses that weigh four tons, consume 100 pounds of food a day, and eat, mate and give birth under water; hyenas, Kenya's most vicious predators, that hunt in packs, can run 40 miles per hour, and have jaws strong enough to bite through bone; leopards, solitary, secretive animals that hunt mainly at night, hang their kill from the tops of trees, and, along with humans, are the only animals that overkill; lions that live in prides of up to 25, hunt in groups, and can run 40 miles per hour, then leap on their prey's back and clamp their jaws on the creature's neck; rhinoceroses that live in families of two to five and are nearly extinct because of poaching; zebras, that stand four feet tall, each with a unique set of stripes that camouflages them in the tall grasses, for their predators are color blind.

The last day of the safari will forever be embedded in my memory. Guests and servants alike began to show symptoms of bacterial dysentery. Stomach cramps, chills, fever and violent diarrhea were visited upon us in turn, and confined us to our hotel room in Nairobi for a week.

Nairobi

The British doctor who came to see us was fascinated by my mother, as a western woman traveling alone with two children is not a common sight in Africa. He was pleased when she accepted his invitation for tea. She was delighted to spend time with a person who would be able to give her an insight into this culture that had so captivated her heart. The tea was served, and the biscuit was barely to his lips when my mother fired her first salvo. "How many servants do you have?" she demanded. He responded that he was a man of modest means and he had a cook and a housekeeper and was about to hire a man to remove the frogs from his garden at night so he could sleep. He told her that servants usually represent the major wage earners for an extended family, and that their wages literally kept the rest of the family alive. He assured my horrified mother that if she lived in Africa, she would probably have twice as many servants and be twice as inventive thinking up things for them to do. What a dilemma that would be for my socialist mother.

After recovering from the terrible dysentery, we were anxious to leave the confines of our hotel room As soon as we could, we set off to explore the remarkable city of Nairobi. I was surprised to see so many very thin men and women who looked both unhappy and unwell. My mother asked a shopkeeper what was wrong with them, and he told her that they were suffering from the "Thin Sickness." That evening we asked the doctor what the Thin Sickness was, and he told us about the rampant spread of AIDS in Kenya. He estimated that at least twenty percent of the newborn infants in Kenya were HIV Positive. He said that due to the lack of education and medicine, the infrequent use of condoms and the tradition of men having many mistresses, AIDS was a major epidemic in Africa. We went to sleep that night thinking about the one in every five infants who would die a painful death, probably before its second birthday.

The Bus Ride

My mother, ever-explaining the sociological significance of the marketplace, dragged us from market to market where we saw people in colorful costumes selling mountains of fruit, nuts and multicolored spices. Small cooking stoves dotted the alleyways and, for a few cents, people could buy skewers of unidentifiable meat. Savory smells from the market joined the sweet fragrances of huge African flowers and all around us people bartered in their lilting and musical languages. The markets were the heart of the city.

We were caught by the night at a market several miles from our hotel. When we boarded the crowded bus to return home, my mother told the driver we were going to the Jacaranda Hotel, and asked him when we should get off. The driver told us to get off at the fourth stop. In fact, he told us twice. We struggled to the back of the bus so we wouldn't miss our stop and two men from the front of the bus followed us. At the back of the bus we stood next to a very tall African man who had a soft smile and gentle eyes. When mom smiled at him, he bowed his head to us. The driver called the fourth stop and the men who had followed us to the back of the bus got off. Mom hesitated on the step because there were no lights at that stop and it was a very dark night. The driver called to her to get off the bus a second time. She hesitated, and looked at the man with the soft smile. Almost imperceptibly, he wrinkled his forehead. The men outside the bus waited. The bus driver called for us to get off a third time. My mom looked at the two men standing outside the bus, hesitated, and told the driver to keep driving. Eventually he moved on. "The next stop," whispered the gentle man. And there it was, a lighted bus stop and a familiar street only three blocks from our hotel.

The next morning, still shaken by the night's bus ride, my mother decided that we would leave Nairobi and travel east to Mombasa. We checked out of our hotel and boarded a bus in record time. It was as if the two men were somehow chasing her.

Mombasa

Five hours later we arrived in Mombasa and checked into a peaceful hotel with a slimy green pool. My mother was finally able to relax and enjoy reading books and writing postcards. Two women braided Zoe's hair into 47 braids, and she looked beautiful. We spent many relaxing days wandering around Mombasa, eating from little sidewalk stands, and making friends with local people and fellow travelers.

Mombasa is the second largest city in Kenya. Because of its deep water port, people from many ethnic backgrounds have settled there. The population is made up of Christians, Hindus and Buddhists, and Africans, Asians and Arabs who are Muslim. Mombasa is the most diverse town in Kenya and you can see that diversity in its many mosques, churches and temples.

Mom asked the owner of a particularly nice shop who sculpted the beautiful animal carvings he sold. With great pride, he directed us to the outskirts of town where dozens of carvers worked under plastic tarps. We watched as the carvers held pieces of wood and, with a few hacks of their hatchets, made giraffes or elephants magically appear. Seconds after putting aside their hatchets and taking out carving knives, the fine detail would emerge. Apprentices placed the carvings in baskets and distributed them to shop owners. While negotiating a price for a small carving of a giraffe for Zoe, we heard about a very special island named Lamu. Two days later we were off to Lamu. To get there, we left our hotel at 5:30 a.m. and took a bus, a small ferry, a taxi, a small plane, another bus and a boat, and it was worth the trip.

Lamu

Lamu is a small island in the Indian Ocean off the cost of Kenya. Arab merchants settled there in the tenth century and intermarried with the Africans. Swahili is the mixture of that Arab and African intermarriage. The old Swahili town, also named Lamu, is over 1,000 years old. The houses are made of stone and thick coral/concrete that gives the buildings a pinkish color and rough texture. The special thing about Lamu is that it is a traditional Islamic community that has twenty active mosques, and at noon on Friday the entire town shuts down for prayers. We were told that followers of Islam from East Africa make a yearly pilgrimage to Lamu.

An intricate web of narrow lanes winds around the old stone buildings. Because they are so narrow, there aren't any cars, buses or trucks on the island. It took my mother about four minutes to get us completely lost in the maze of lanes. Eventually we found a small marketplace and, after waving our hands around for a while, were

86

able to buy some fruit for lunch. A few hours later I asked my mom how we were going to get back to the port in time to catch the boat, bus, small plane, taxi, small ferry and other bus that would take us back to Mombasa. She responded that since we were on an island we would just look for the water. The fact that we hadn't seen water for the last half hour didn't seem to bother her as she smiled at the black-veiled women who seemed to appear and as quickly disappear from the very stone walls. Much later, in front of the same mosque that we had somehow passed three times, my mother began to worry about how we would get back. It was getting late and we had no map, but even if we did have one there were no street signs.

While Zoe played ball with five little kids, mom and I sat on the steps of the mosque and tried to come up with a plan. "Thor, ask the kids to take us to the water," my mother suggested. Since the kids spoke no English, and Zoe's newly acquired vocabulary in Swahili was of absolutely no help, I knew it wasn't going to be easy. I went up to the children and pointed to myself, my mom and Zoe, and shrugged my shoulders. They seemed to understand because they smiled and shook their heads in agreement. Then one of the kids threw the ball to me so I could join the game. My mother's laughter was absolutely no help at all. I tried again. I gave the ball back to the boy who had thrown it to me. I pointed to myself, mom and Zoe, then I pointed what might have been north, east, south and west, and rapidly shrugged my shoulders about six times. Even though Zoe and mom were just about rolling around on the ground laughing, the kids got the idea we were lost. The oldest boy grabbed Zoe's hand and pulled her down a street. Mom and I, and a dozen children who seemed to multiply after every turn, ran behind them. We turned left, then right, then left and left and left again and came to a winding lane that was so narrow that the walls brushed our shoulders as we ran through it. A few turns later we were suddenly at the dock. As mom rewarded the kids with sweets and change, I helped Zoe into the last boat that would leave the island that night—it was leaving in a minute and a half.

PERU

Zoe is ten and I am eighteen.

The morning we were to leave for Peru, an advisory came from the American government warning us not to go there because the Sendero Luminoso, the "Shining Path" (a guerrilla organization), was murdering American tourists. I told my mother that we should listen to the warning and stay home. She replied that there would be far fewer tourists, and wouldn't that be nice. In three hours, we were on a plane for Lima. Later that summer, a Peruvian university professor told us the American government had sent out the travel advisory because Peru was defaulting on their debt payments. He said that keeping American tourists at home was a ploy to get Peru to resume those payments.

Lima

We arrived late at night at an airport that was in chaos because it had been bombed the day before. There were so few tourists, and the cab drivers were so frantic for fares, that several of them reached for our canvas bag in an effort to drag us to their cab. My mother, clutching our bag for dear life, called out, "Chi parla Italiano?" (Who speaks Italian?) She always spoke in Italian when in a tight situation in a foreign country.

An Italian-looking man answered, "Sono Italiano," (I am Italian) and we jumped into his cab. The cab driver told us it was very dangerous to be on the streets of Lima so late at night, and he pointed out the bullet holes in the walls of the airport. I asked him if the Shining Path had put them there. When he said they hadn't, I was somehow relieved.   My mom told him we would be flying to the Amazon in eight hours, but we were tired and she was afraid to stay in the airport. I think she was more afraid of the other cab drivers than of the people who had put the bullet holes in the walls. The cab driver understood and drove us to his sister's house where we slept soundly for six hours until he returned to drive us back to the airport. We were exhausted.

At the airport, I made a bed for my sister by pushing our canvas bag and my pack together. I spread her on top of them and she immediately fell asleep with her head at an odd angle to avoid a zipper. Mom covered her with a jacket, and Zoe slept soundly for two hours while we joined fourteen angry passengers who were yelling at the ticket agent who had mis-booked our plane and stranded us at the Lima airport. We were on our way to the Tambopata Reserve on the Amazon River, deep in the Peruvian Jungle.

The Amazon
We finally boarded an old twin-engine Russian Antinov with aluminum tape on its wings. Once airborne, my mother came to life and awakened her children who were comatose with exhaustion. There, far below our wings, a silver thread meandered through the dense jungle — the Amazon.

After an horrific flight that made most of the passengers airsick, we landed on what must have been the world's shortest runway. We joined the other first-time passengers who screamed as the plane took a dive, and at the last minute banked steeply, landed and nearly collided with the trees at the end of the runway. After getting off the airplane, we looked around for the Tambopata Reserve. It wasn't there. Ten of the passengers disappeared into the jungle, and the plane took off leaving seven of us looking at each other. Eventually, someone found a man sleeping in a truck with a sign that read Tambopata Reserve. We thought we had arrived, but we hadn't.

Once awakened the man herded us into the back of his pick-up truck, and we took off on a merciless trek through the jungle. Three hours later we were on the shore of the great river, a long, thin dugout canoe with an outboard motor before us. Again we thought we had arrived, but we hadn't. Passengers were loaded into the bow, luggage and supplies into the stern. A man on the shore beat bunches of bananas with sticks before loading them.

"Porque?" (why?) asked my mother.
"Tarantulas," answered the man with the stick.

Cringing, and as far away from the bananas as possible, we boarded the long canoe called a teca after the "teca-teca-teca" sound of the motor and headed 36 miles upriver to Tambopata. The pilot asked my mother not to trail her bandana in the water as it alerted the piranha and the small crocodiles called caimans. Zoe and I laughed at the look on her face as she quickly removed it.

The reserve consisted of a very large, circular meeting-dining room with bamboo walls and a thatched roof. A row of small rooms outfitted with laboratory equipment stretched to the east of the circular room. To the west were half a dozen small bamboo huts joined by a bamboo boardwalk. Another bamboo walk crossed the clearing to the boat launch. Our first of many warnings was not to step off the boardwalks onto the clearing.

Guests and scientists ate dinner together in the evening and were encouraged to help themselves to the ample pile of fruit for breakfast and lunch. My mother trusted nothing but the bananas for, in her words, "they come pre-wrapped." We were encouraged to ask any of the scientists at the table permission to go with them into the jungle. All of them were most anxious to share their work and talk with anyone from the world beyond the reserve. Just what my mother wanted, an entomologist of her own who would explain the fragility of this vast ecosystem to her children.

The next morning was intensely hot and humid. Shortly after breakfast, we met the entomologist we would accompany into the jungle. He instructed us how to fold our pants into our socks to protect us from the ants. We wore long-sleeved shirts, and covered our hands, necks and faces with insect repellent. He warned us not to touch anything that looked like a rope, for in the Amazon Jungle some of the snakes are covered with moss and look exactly like old ropes. He told us to look for boa constrictors that hung on low limbs and fell on their prey. The entomologist pointed out that this reserve was the richest in the world in its biodiversity. It held the world record for the number of bird species, 572, many of which had been previously unrecorded. He said that more than 1,200 species of butterflies had been recorded there. In two and a half acres, 150 types of trees had been recorded, and on a single leguminous tree, 43 species of ants were discovered, equal to the entire ant fauna of the British Isles.

We learned that most of the tropical species are found in the foliage of the forest canopy, the interlacing tops of the trees. The majority of them never descend during their lifetimes. It is a challenge for scientists to catalog them because they are suspended 50 meters above the ground. At best, we can only glimpse into the biomass that comprises this ecosystem. An entomologist once shot insecticide into the tree canopy and nearly every species of insect that was recovered had never been seen before. In one hectare of the Peruvian Amazon forest 41,000 species had been identified.

The entomologist laughed at our sunglasses and warned us that the light would diminish by 86% six paces into the forest. My mother, thirteen-year-old Zoe and I took off our sunglasses, and we set foot on the path that would lead us to the most diversified ecosystem on our planet.

We stepped into the rain forest—dark. A few feet further— darker. Beckoned by darkness we walked on. Sounds overwhelmed us. Things fell from trees. My footstep startled something and it slithered out of a log. Something short and furry crossed the path to chase it. Birds cawed, screamed, whistled and growled. Fluorescent butterflies the size of small frisbees passed within inches of our faces. We stopped near a 90-foot philodendron with four-foot leaves to watch a regiment of army ants detour around a three-foot termite mound. The entomologist busied himself coaxing something into a jar while insects circled our heads in vain trying to find a repellent-free place to land. We continued on—darker, deeper, farther, louder, noisier, greener, deeper, darker. A different kind of hot now, a green hot born from the struggle of survival as insects and animals fed on each other for sustenance, and plants climbed upon and killed each other in an effort to reach the sun. Never silent, and in constant motion, the forest breathed and pulsated, lived and died in the humid heat.

Above the canopy the wind blew and a 70-foot tree swayed, disturbing its upper canopy of leaves and allowing a spear of light to fall on the forest floor. Just enough light to ensure a vine another day's survival, another millimeter up the tree that robbed its sun, another millimeter to the top of the canopy where it would spread itself and eventually kill the shallow-rooted tree that provided its access. When the tree fell, it would bring down and bury the vine that killed it. A fallen tree allowed a shaft of light into the jungle which would allow another tree to grow, and the process would begin again.

As we stood in awe of the struggle for light, the jungle exploded around us. A crash to our right, then to our left, another behind us. What came down must have come from up I thought, and there in a tree a monkey, and then another, and another and another, throwing nuts at us. We stood, they sat, we looked at each other. Zoe and I whistled hello, unconsciously translating our words into jungle sounds. I was momentarily distracted as an iridescent frisbee of a butterfly hiccupped past me, barely missing an angry-sounding three-inch flying beetle, guided by an unseen air traffic controller. I stepped back and the yellow, green and blue lizard that had come to examine my boot scampered back into the darkness of the jungle.

We spent many days in that most mysterious jungle, and every day we experienced the world around us with new eyes. Even the tiniest insect was fascinating. We watched a trail of ants climb a tree, cut out sections of leaves that were five times taller than they were, and return them to their nest where they would use the leaves to fertilize fungi, their only food source. We saw a battalion of army ants on the move. At night they would form living nests by circling their queen and forming a live pyramid of ants above her. We saw a bird with a neck that looked like a multicolored feather duster; it made a sound like a woman being stabbed while yodeling. And everywhere we went, curious monkeys trailed behind us and threw nuts at us to get our attention. When we felt capable to go into the forest without the entomologist, he told us to fashion a stick into an arrow. The moment we stopped on the path we were to place the arrow on the ground pointing the direction we were traveling. The Amazon jungle was so dense that if we stopped and looked around, we would have no idea which way we had come and which way we were going, and would have no idea which way to go to return to the camp.

One morning, in an effort to get to our hut before my mom and Zoe, I took a short cut from the dining hall and, avoiding the bamboo walkway, ran across the clearing. By that evening my legs and ankles were covered with chigger bites (a mite larva that lodges in the skin and bites, causing severe itching). While my mother was trying to figure out what a chigger was, and how to tend to the welts they caused, my sister approached with a banana in her hand. "Who took a big bite out of the center?" she asked. More concerned about my legs than the banana, my mom put it on a small shelf. That night we were awakened by a scratching sound. We whispered to each other and simultaneously shone our flashlights toward the sound of the scratching. There on the shelf, taking another bite out of the banana was a very large bamboo rat.

We were so lucky to have experienced this most magical place. However, the pressure of cutting trees for quick foreign revenue, clearing land for agriculture and cattle ranching, poaching and gold mining, makes the protection of this unguarded reserve extremely difficult. The entomologist told us that the accelerating destruction of the world's rain forests is considered by biologists a global crisis. The tropical rain forests contain 60% of all the species on earth, yet occupy only seven percent of the land surface. Annually, two million acres are lost, eliminating forever 20,000 species. He told us that we do not know what affect that will have on the complex interaction between air, water, soil and living things. We do not know which plants might have the potential to cure the diseases that plague us today, and those which will plague us tomorrow.

Cuzco

The return flight from the Amazon to Lima was every bit as harrowing as the arrival had been. This time, however, we were already broken in and nobody screamed when the landing gear skimmed the tops of the trees upon take off. Within forty-five minutes of landing at the Lima Airport, we were on a plane to Cuzco. The connection was remarkably easy, perhaps due to the battalion of worried-looking soldiers that were hurrying the passengers along. If my pacifist mother was upset by the guards with bayonets on their rifles, she didn't make a fuss. Many very nervous passengers asked the flight attendant all kinds of questions, but her response to all of them was, " Would you like coffee, tea or juice from the apple fruit?"

A couple of hours and 686 miles later, we landed in Cuzco, a small city tucked into the southeast corner of the Andes. The airport didn't seem to be under siege, and everyone looked pretty normal, with the exception of my mother who lacked the enthusiasm she always had when coming to a new city. We stowed our pack and canvas bag at our hotel and took a small bus to the Temple of the Sun, an ancient Inca ruin. From the window of the bus we could see Cuzco's diverse culture. The architecture showed the influence of the Spanish colonials, and the people dressed in colorful clothes were an Inca and European mixture. Zoe pointed out a donkey-drawn cart filled with laughing children driven by a very old man with a flower in his straw hat. Normally such a scene would cause our mother to lunge for the camera, but all she managed was a slight smile.

The Temple of the Sun was very impressive. Huge slabs of stones were so delicately placed together that wind and rain could not erode their bond. Watching the bright Peruvian sun play off the eleventh-century walls made it easy to imagine that we were at the very center of the Inca empire.

There were few tourists in Cuzco because most Americans had heeded the State Department's warnings. That morning we were alone at the Temple of the Sun. My mom told me she was going to rest for a while. She asked me to take Zoe to explore the ruins, and to pay special attention to the construction of the walls. When Zoe called out that she had found a statue of a strange looking beast, I ran down an ancient stone pathway to join her.

I found out later that while we were enjoying ourselves in that magical place, our mother was vomiting on an intricately constructed Pre-Colombian stairway. She staggered to the shade of a small tree and was sitting under it with her head in her hands when a native Quechua woman walked by.

"Hola," (hello) said my very green-looking mother.
"¿Qué pasa?" (What is wrong?) asked the woman
"Mi cabeza, mi estómago," (my head, my stomach) my mother replied.

The woman reached into the recesses of her colorful woven shawl and pulled out some green leaves which she crumbled between her palms. She then placed her strong, broad, callused hands over my mother's face and said "respire, respire" (breathe, breathe). After a few deep breaths, my mother's nausea receded slightly, and she was able to point to her forehead, move her head back and forth, and somehow communicate to the woman that she felt very dizzy.

A small leather pouch materialized next, and the woman pulled a brown sticky chunk of something out of it. She rolled the substance in her hands and told my mother to open her mouth. Under normal circumstances my mother would never place anything that wasn't certifiably free of dysentery-ridden bacteria into her mouth. But these were in no way normal circumstances. Her children were out of her sight for the first time in weeks, and she was too weak to stand. Without a shred of objection, she welcomed the woman's dirty fingers into her mouth and allowed the brown sticky chunk to be placed between her cheek and her lower right molar. Realizing she had come to the end of my mother's meager Spanish vocabulary, the woman made a chewing motion with her teeth and shook her head sideways. The message was clear—don't chew.

When my mother opened her eyes half an hour later, the woman was gone, and Zoe and I were shaking her and calling her name. After a few minutes, Mom began to look a little better, but she still didn't look good. I left Zoe with her and hailed one of the cabs that cruised the ruins.

By the time we arrived at the hotel, mom wasn't looking any worse but she wasn't making any sense. She smiled at the hotel clerk who was standing in front of the elevator, told him that our room was on the third floor, and asked him where the third floor was. He must have thought she was drunk because when he opened the elevator door for us he smiled at her and pointed up. The creaking elevator came to a stop on the third floor and the door opened. My mother staggered into the hall, dropped her purse and began to sink to the floor. I caught her and Zoe grabbed her purse and unlocked the door to our room.

We put our mother on the bed. I tried to explain to her that Zoe was going to stay with her and I was going to get a doctor, but her eyes showed us she didn't understand. I ran down the stairs to the front desk because I didn't want to chance another bad elevator. The clerk called a doctor and followed me back to our room with a portable oxygen tank. "No está a borracha," (She isn't drunk) he said. "Tiene mal de altitud." (She has altitude sickness.) He turned the oxygen on and put the mask on my mom's face. She drank in the oxygen as if she were thirsty. I tried to make her understand that the hotel kept oxygen for tourists who became ill from altitude sickness, and this time I thought she understood a bit of what I was saying. Later she told me that she recognized all my words, but she was unable to put them into any kind of coherent order.

A few minutes later our mother began to vomit profusely. Just as I was telling Zoe not to be afraid because the doctor was coming, the thank-God-he-spoke-English doctor arrived. The doctor asked us how we had come to Cuzco, where we had been before that, if our mother had been ill before she landed in Cuzco, when her symptoms had begun and how they had progressed. After examining her, he became quite concerned about the severity of her altitude sickness and told me he was going to administer injections of Dramamine and

Diamox. I told him I hoped he wouldn't consider me rude, but I wanted to examine his syringes before he injected my mother. When he produced sterile, packaged syringes, I nodded my approval.

A few minutes after the injections our mother was considerably better. The doctor told me we had to leave Cuzco immediately because the 11,207-foot altitude had made our mother extremely ill, and she could get worse very quickly. He suggested we take the train to Machu Picchu that was leaving early the next morning. I asked him if he would accept American Express travelers checks, and told him that I could forge my mom's signature on them because we both could see she was unable to hold a pen. The doctor surprised me by shaking my hand and telling me that he wasn't going to charge us anything because he was so impressed that I had asked to see his syringes. He gave Zoe a little hug, patted me on the back and left. We were on our way to Machu Picchu the next morning.

After a four-hour, 80-kilometer train ride and a descent of 2,000 feet we boarded a bus that took us on a hair-raising zig-zagging ride far too close to the edge of the steep mountain road. It seemed that every foot we descended our mother came back to life a little. The moment she could compose a coherent sentence, she asked the bus driver what the woman had put into her mouth. "Coca," he replied. "The cocaine helps the peasants work long hours in the high altitude. It speeds up their heart rate so they get more oxygen." When he heard how ill my mom had become, he added that without the cocaine she probably wouldn't have made it back to the hotel.

Machu Picchu

One of the greatest moments in archeological history occurred in 1911 when Hiram Binghan, an archaeologist from Yale University, discovered the lost City of the Incas— Machu Picchu. This citadel sits upon a high plateau, its massive pre-Columbian ruins extending for five square miles. Once again, to our delight, we found very few tourists so the ruins were almost completely ours to explore.

There is something beckoning about the ruins of Machu Picchu. Every morning we stood in them and watched the sun rise, just as the Inca Children of the Sun must have done long ago. It's difficult to write about these magnificent ruins because it seems as if the words should be whispered. Many times Zoe, mom, and I found ourselves completely alone, surrounded by ruins that were themselves surrounded by the Andes Mountains—whispering to each other.

The slabs and blocks of granite that made this fortress city were joined in mortarless joints so tightly that a piece of paper cannot be slid between them. Three thousand gray granite steps link intricate terraces where enough food was grown to feed the entire population of the city. The people of Machu Picchu ate corn that had, for the first time in history, been purposely crossbred and genetically altered.

The terraces and a series of natural springs made Machu Picchu completely self-sufficient. Huge blocks, many weighing fifty tons, were used in the construction of palaces, temples, baths, storage rooms and 150 houses. A sun clock that indicates special dates sat at the center of an astronomical observatory. The conquering Spaniards never found Machu Picchu, for it is completely invisible from below.

One would have thought that my mother, who was usually delighted by anthropological and architectural wonders, would have been resonating with joy in this most magnificent setting—but she wasn't. Instead, she seemed distracted and a bit nervous.

Several days later, Zoe and I remained at the hotel near the ruins while my mother joined three women and climbed Huayna Picchu, the most photographed peak in that area. After the hike, she spent the evening alone in the ruins. At dusk, when she returned to the hotel, she told us that while alone in the ruins she realized that horrible Inca sacrifices had been made there. The ground had been soaked with women's blood she said, and she wanted to leave Machu Picchu as soon as possible. That night, her dreams were about blood, sacrifice and death.

Since the bus didn't leave until late afternoon the next day, I got up at dawn and climbed Huayna Picchu. Zoe told me she read a book and mom paced back and forth nervously until I returned. Days later we came across the three women mom had climbed with, and they told us that each of them had horrible dreams that same night. They all felt that some sort of brutal sacrifices had occurred at Machu Picchu and they all left as soon as they could. For the first time in our travels, my mom was ready to go home.

ECUADOR
Zoe is eleven and I am nineteen

The first thing I noticed about Ecuador was that the children looked healthier and the dogs looked fatter and better cared for than they did in Peru. We were told that because the Andes Mountains ran through Peru, it had less arable land. The topsoil was deeper in Ecuador making it easier to grow crops, and that's why the children and the animals were better fed. Ecuador is the size of the state of Colorado. It spans the Equator and runs from snow-capped mountains to the Amazon Jungle, with arable land between. Six hundred miles off its coast lie the Galapagos Islands.

Quito, the capital of Ecuador, is on a plateau surrounded by snow-capped mountains. The city is filled with beautiful cathedrals, elegant mansions and interesting museums, but when my mom found out that the most famous market in South America was two hours north, in the town of Otavalo, she made plans to go there the next day.

The night before we left for Otavalo, we discovered a restaurant a few blocks from our hotel that served pizza. Knowing that we would be eating a variety of ethnic food for the next two months, mom took us there. Thinking that the pizzas were small, we ordered two of them, and were surprised when the waiter covered the table with two large pizzas. We had eaten our fill and still had one and a half pizzas left when a little boy walked up to my mother. "Chicklets," he said. "Quiere comprar Chicklets?" (Do you want to buy Chicklets?) The little boy who wasn't much more than six years old was dressed in dirty rags and had no shoes. In one hand he held a small cardboard box that held about twenty small packets of Chicklets gum in it. With the other hand he held a homespun shawl over his back. "Que tienes?" (What do you have?) my mother asked as she pointed to the shawl.

When the little guy didn't answer, my mother gently turned him around to take a look for herself. The first thing she saw was a small foot sticking out from the bulk of the shawl. "Oh God, a baby," my mother gasped. "Buy all the Chicklets, Thor!" she said, and as Zoe took the box from the child my mother unwrapped the baby. The infant was about nine months old and looked as if she was in reasonable health. The woolen diaper she wore was soaked and the child was asleep. Without the little boy seeing her, my mother folded money into the infant's homemade diaper and rewrapped her in the shawl. "¿A tí te gusta pizza?" (Do you like pizza?) she asked the little boy, and his eyes shone. We asked the waiter to wrap the pizza for him so that he could carry it with one hand, and we watched the little boy run down the street with it.

When Zoe asked why that baby wasn't at home with its mother, our traumatized mother answered that its mother was probably a woman in prostitution who was working the streets at night. She told us that we had witnessed a powerful picture of poverty and we should remember that when we returned to our comfortable home, that little boy would still be here selling Chicklets, that little baby would still be wrapped up in a shawl on his back, and their mother would still be working on the streets. She explained that there are cycles of poverty that are nearly impossible to break out of, and we had just witnessed one of them.

On our way home we walked by a doorway and saw the little boy and three of his friends enjoying the pizza, the shawl, containing the baby, on the sidewalk near their feet. "Hola Señora," called the little boy. "Hola," we all called back.

Otavalo

A two-hour shuttle-bus ride took us from Quito to Otavalo and deposited us on the steps of a hacienda that was well over 200 years old. The hacienda stood in sharp contrast to the roach-filled hotel we had slept in the night before. The rooms were spacious, the floors were tiled, and great beamed ceilings spanned the large dining and living rooms. We could tell that this had been the home of a very rich and powerful Spanish lord before the revolution. We slept like babies in the spacious beds until our mother awakened us at 6:00 a.m. to go to the Saturday market at Poncho Plaza.

At 6:30 Zoe and I were stumbling down a dirt road after our energized mother who kept telling us to hurry, we were almost there, because she could hear the pigs squealing. A bend in the road later we were there! The market was alive — pigs squealing, dogs barking, donkeys braying, chickens clucking and Indian men, women and children calling to each other. Natives from the surrounding mountains came to town every Saturday to sell their crafts, produce and livestock at this market. You could buy almost anything. There were textiles, baskets, ponchos, cows, goats, pigs, leatherwork, tapestries, hats, cheeses, horses, chickens—and skinned calves heads. The delicious smell of baking bread made us hungry, even though the meat stalls covered with blood, severed hooves, eyeballs and fly-covered carcasses were a vegetarian's hell.

Mom told us that this was perhaps the most authentic market in South America. The Indians spoke Quechua, their native language, and wore traditional dress that dated back to their Inca ancestors. The women wore white blouses, blue skirts and shawls and adorned themselves with layers of gold and coral necklaces and bracelets. The men wore blue ponchos, white knickers and fedoras. Their long black braids came to their waists.

Hours later, we sat on a little hill overlooking the market and ate some of the fresh produce and delicious bread our mother had bought for lunch. We were in a truly amazing place, tall volcanoes surrounding us, and sounds from the colorful marketplace wafting toward us. "I can't even remember what my bedroom at home looks like," said Zoe for, like mom and me, she too was transported by the sights, smells and sounds to ancient Incan times.

We left Otavalo a few days later and took a bus that led us first through vast plantations of roses that would be exported all over the world and then to a village of weavers. The Incas, having no alphabet, communicated concepts about seasonal time, architectural practices and history through their weaving. The men and women of this town, descendants of the Incan weavers, cleaned, spun, dyed and spooled yarn. Skilled hands pushed shuttles back and forth and wove symbols and designs that dated back to ancestral times. The very old and the very young worked side by side as they had for centuries.

We spent the night in a lesser hacienda in a small rural village. We slept late because we were exhausted. The next morning we were awakened by cheering people and banging drums. Within minutes, our mother had us dressed and running down a dirt road after the parade. It was July 24, and this was Fiestas Patrias, (Independence Day). The town folk and Indians from the neighboring slopes had all come dressed in their best traditional costumes, formed a parade and were winding their way to the town square. Women were laughing and singing and men were banging on drums and playing brass instruments that sounded as if they had been run over by a donkey cart. Mom ran to the front of the parade to photograph it, but instead just stood there with her mouth open. Zoe and I were just as stunned when we saw the five women leading the parade swinging live chickens over their heads. The parade ended in the small town square. People were laughing and hugging each other and drinking lots of wine out of goatskin pouches — the chickens were dead. While the young women twirled in circles and their skirts and braids fanned out around them, young men fired rifles into the air. "Grab your sister," said my mother, "we're getting out of here."

When the manager of the hacienda came back from the parade, he filled us in on some Ecuadorian history. In the 11th century, the Inca Empire included Ecuador. A network of roads and temples united the 400,000-square-mile Inca Nation that extended from Southern Columbia to northwest Argentina. At the height of its power a nine-yard-wide road, called the Inca Highway, crossed over 100 rivers and streams and led from Cuzco in Peru to Quito in Ecuador. In 1526, Pizarro landed and the Conquistadors laid waste to this noble civilization and enslaved its people. In 1822, Simon Bolivar liberated

Ecuador from Spanish rule, and they now celebrate Independence Day on his birthday.

In preparation for our return to Quito, my mother was washing our clothes in a small sink. After she pulled the plug, the water stagnated a while and the basin slowly emptied. She complained about the sluggish drains as she had for the two months we had been in Ecuador. I told her that in the northern hemisphere the draining water swirls counter-clockwise, in the southern hemisphere the draining water swirls clockwise, but at the equator the water doesn't swirl at all and that's why it moves so slowly. I explained to her that vines do the same thing, counter-clockwise above the equator and clockwise below it. "So how come you took two months to tell me!" she said and she threw a bunch of soggy socks at me.

THE GALAPAGOS ISLANDS
Zoe is twelve and I am twenty

Because we traveled on a mercilessly tight budget, my mother was always looking for travel bargains. In Africa, we traveled in a small bus we lovingly called "Bottom-of-the-Barrel Safaris." In Australia, we went on the last bus-camping trip a soon-to-be-defunct travel company would ever run. Of the many boats that toured the Galapagos Islands, my mother found the one with the least expensive rates. The moment we left the dock, the captain retreated to his quarters and was never seen again, the cooks kept asking any of the twenty passengers who weren't actively vomiting over the rail if they would help in the kitchen, and the crew was on the brink of mutiny. The discontent aboard our boat, however, did nothing to dampen the excitement we felt as we traveled the Galapagos Islands.

We visited seven of the islands, traveling from one to another mostly at night. The water was particularly rough that summer, and our relatively small vessel was pitched and tossed about. I became seasick for a while. My mother wore a scopolamine disk that kept her from becoming seasick but made her a bit strange. She kept coming up to me and saying, "Excuse me Thor, be sure to hold onto the rail very tightly so you wouldn't fall overboard while vomiting." Zoe spent a lot of time in the kitchen with the cooks making pancakes for the dwindling number of people who could eat breakfast.

The Galapagos Islands were formed by volcanic activity, and numerous hot spots indicate they are still the most volcanic islands in the world. They lie 600 miles west of Ecuador's coastline, and are a world heritage site because of the uniqueness of their plants and animals. In order to protect their fragile ecosystems, visitors are asked not to step off the paths that crisscross the islands. The animals and birds we encountered had never been hunted and, therefore, had no natural fear of humans. Many times we had to step around nests of blue-footed boobies, white gull-like birds with bright blue feet, who pecked at our sandaled feet when we stepped too close to their eggs.

Charles Darwin came to the Galapagos Islands in 1845, and was the first biologist to explore them. On these unique islands, he was able to observe species of animals that had evolved in isolation. The conclusions he drew from his observations led him to propose the theory of natural selection and evolution, which led to his book *The Origin of the Species*. How these incredibly unique animals adapted to their hostile environment has revolutionized how we think about life.

"Galapagos" means giant turtle, and it is little wonder these islands were named after these most remarkable beasts. We visited the Charles Darwin Research Station, and giant tortoises that weighed up to 500 pounds, whose shells measured four feet across and who live to be 150 years old, lumbered past us. The tortoise population was severely depleted by the 19th century because whaling ships stacked them in their hulls storing them there alive until they were ready to eat them at sea. Today, the threat of hungry whalers has been replaced by the threat of wild goats. In the early 19th century, four goats were brought to the islands. At the end of the 20th century 100,000 feral goats became such a threat to other species that the goat extinction project was instituted. These goats eat the tall grasses that protect the tortoises from the sun, and exposure to the sun causes them to overheat and die.

One day, while walking along a desolate beach, we saw six baby tortoises crawl down a sandy slope and make a mad rush for the sea. Large birds circled over them, and, if it weren't for Zoe yelling, screaming, waving her hands and jumping all over the place, the baby tortoises would have been scooped up by the birds. As the last of the tortoises made it to the sea and Zoe collapsed on the sand, I reminded her that they were probably being eaten by the sea creatures that lie in wait for the ones that make it past the birds. A female tortoise will lay many eggs, but very few of them ever make it to adulthood because of the birds, rats and fish that feed on them. Zoe kicked sand into the water and stormed down the beach.

We walked toward a series of lava flows that seemed to pulsate, and were surprised to find they were covered by marine iguanas lying in the morning sun to raise their body temperature. When the iguanas became too warm, they would crawl into the water to cool down and eat marine lettuce. These gentle, prehistoric-looking iguanas with barnacles growing on their heads blended into the rock so well that Zoe almost sat on one that was four feet long. The iguanas shared the lava flows with lava lizards that blended in with the color of the rock and sand on each island—red on one, gray on another, a bit greenish on a third.

On the nights that we weren't traveling from island to island, we anchored in small, protected bays. Before we fell asleep, Mom, Zoe and I would talk about what we enjoyed the most that day. Mom liked the red-footed boobies that laid a single egg that was tended by both the mother and father boobie. Zoe liked the great frigate birds—long, jet black birds that swooped, dove and flew within feet of us, and whose mating dance consisted of puffing air into bright red sacks below their beaks that would expand to look like large, red balloons. Mom and I laughed when Zoe told us how much she disliked a gecko that hissed at her. I liked the cormorants that had evolved to the point where they no longer flew, but instead swam using their wings to steer and their feet to pedal. We fell asleep on those wonderful nights under an unfamiliar sky, with gentle waves lapping against the hull of our boat, looking forward to the next day of adventure.

Every day was exciting. Swallow-tailed gulls, warblers, cactus finches, doves and mockingbirds serenaded us as we walked along the thin paths gently indented into the lava flows. The ocean water was rich in nutrients and everything seemed so alive in that desolate place devoid of any buildings. We sat on a sandy spot near rocks that were completely covered with sea urchins and watched lava herons, just a few feet away from us, feed on small fish, rock crabs and lizards. We could spend hours looking at small calderas, caldron-like indentations in the rock made by volcanic spews, teaming with life.

One day, we joined four other people and paddled a dinghy through the mangrove swamps on one of the islands. The water was crystal clear and teamed with multicolored fish. We steered through small passageways and ducked under branches while schools of golden rays fluttered under our boat and the occasional shark meandered by.

The most fun we had was on the days we spent sunning ourselves on the white sand beaches and snorkeling with the seals and sea lions. The beaches were so covered with sea lions that we had to walk around and over them to get to the blue-green water. The waters were clear and warm and were teaming with vividly colored and incredibly friendly fish. While I admired a parrotfish with bright orange eyes, I saw Zoe swimming with a baby sea lion. The curious pup kept bumping its nose against Zoe's mask, which would cause Zoe to laugh so hard that her mask would leak and she would need to surface to readjust it. The pup played with Zoe for quite a while, first bumping her mask, then pulling at her flippers. The awkward penguins that lumbered down the beach with Charlie-Chaplin-like steps became jet propelled as soon as they hit the water. Using their wings as flippers they flew through the water and negotiated right-angle turns without slowing down.

After Zoe's playmate swam away, she lay down on the beach near a group of four mother and four baby sea lions. I joined her and lay my blanket next to hers. A few minutes later a male sea lion approached us, made a strange puffing sound and flapped his flippers on the sand. He was still for a minute or two, then slowly approached me and gently bit me on my thigh. If I hadn't been wearing spandex his gentle bite would have drawn blood, but because of the layer of extra skin the spandex afforded me, I suffered only two long bruises. The male sea lion quickly got between Zoe and me and pushed me away from her. Evidently, she was now part of his family and I had been expelled.

The explorers of old call the Galapagos "the enchanted islands" because they can be suddenly obscured by thick, low sea mists, and sometimes, when the mists shift, the islands themselves appear to move. But these islands are enchanted for another reason, for nowhere in the world can people walk with such impunity amid fearless animals and birds, some of which can be found nowhere else in the world. Perhaps this series of desolate volcanic islands is the true Garden of Eden.

CONCLUSION

by Zoe Dehr Curylo

Our travels began when I was two years old, and continued until I was thirteen. When people ask me if I regret having traveled at such a young age, the answer is always no. Had I been older, I would have remembered names and places better, and sometimes I regret not being able to do that. However, being so young I was able to experience each country with very little cultural bias.

I never experience culture shock because I grew up understanding how varied the world is. I didn't abstractly learn about different cultures, I experienced them. At five years old, I saw five-year-olds who were starving. There was no difference between me and the little girls I played with—only that they were more hungry than I, and the most sturdy wall in their house was an old, dirty mattress standing on end.

Children are not born with set values. Their value systems come from their parents, the society in which they live and the environment they experience. As a young child I experienced many cultures in the third world. At a young age, I witnessed first hand what prejudice, intolerance, injustice and poverty can do. It was those remarkable experiences that helped to mold both my character and my values. I have always found the time to stand up for the disenfranchised, and for people who have no voice. I think that having experienced the third world as a child has made me a far better person.

by Thor Dehr

What an amazing experience it has been to visit so many different countries and learn about the people who live there through first-hand experiences. My mother was our teacher—and the world was our classroom. Traveling the world and meeting its people has made me understand that there are far fewer absolutes than most of us realize. Our travels have given my sister and me a unique perspective on lifestyles, beliefs and even the nature of our existence. We learned to understand poverty and to respect people whose ways were vastly different from ours. We learned what a privilege it is to be born in and to live in North America.

During our childhoods, Zoe and I spent our summers traveling and photographing foreign countries. As adults we unconsciously, but perhaps inevitably, continued those pursuits. Zoe moved through a series of varied careers, from heavy truck mechanic to being an accomplished equestrian. She is now a photographer. Zoe both sees and interprets the world through her viewfinder.

While in college I thought seriously about becoming a doctor or a lawyer. But the joy I experienced while traveling led me to get a degree in aerospace and I became a professional pilot. Traveling the world is my work, and I see the world through an airplane window.

Thank you mom,
Zoe and Thor

111